My Church Is *Not* Dying

EPISCOPALIANS IN THE 21ST CENTURY

+>•••<+

Greg Garrett

MP Morehouse Publishing
NEW YORK

Morehouse Publishing, 19 East 34th Street, New York, NY 10016

Morehouse Publishing is an imprint of Church Publishing Incorporated.
www.churchpublishing.org

Cover design by Laurie Klein Westhafer
Typeset by PerfecType, Nashville, TN

Library of Congress Cataloging-in-Publication Data
Garrett, Greg.
  My church is not dying : Episcopalians in the 21st century / Greg Garrett.
    pages cm
  Includes bibliographical references.
  ISBN 978-0-8192-2934-2 (pbk.) -- ISBN 978-0-8192-2935-9 (ebook) 1. Church renewal.
2. Episcopal Church. I. Title.
  BX5933.G37 2015
  283'.7309051--dc23

                              2014043046

Printed in the United States of America

Contents

Foreword: The Right Reverend Greg Rickel   ix

Introduction: My Church Is Not Dying   1

The Anglican Way: Spiritual and Religious   19

Living the Questions: A Faith That Stays Open All Night   35

Worship and Community: One Way God Touches and Heals Us   47

Beauty and the Life of God: Music, Culture,
    and the Incarnate Way   61

Living Together: How the Culture Wars Almost Killed Us—
    But Made Us Stronger   77

Telling the World: Evangelism for a World That Hates Evangelism
    but Needs the Church   89

Doing Justice: A Church That Works   103

Reaching Out: Touching Lives All Week Long   121

Author's Note   139

Notes   141

About the Author   145

For the Episcopal Church,
and all who love her

Don't let your heart grow cold.
I will call you by name.
I will share your road.

✦ ✦ ✦

Mumford and Sons, *Babel*

Foreword

Compline is an ancient monastic office. For many it is old school, destined to be gone soon. Yet, at St. Mark's Cathedral in Seattle it has gone on just about every Sunday night for fifty-eight years. Currently there are no signs of its demise. In fact, a normal Sunday night will see five hundred to seven hundred people, most of them under thirty, who show up at 9:30 p.m. to be reverently present for the exactly thirty-minute chanted service. Taking part in this experience cannot help but move you. When the choristers leading the prayers come to the Creed, everyone in the place stands. Many do not know why, but they do it. When the Creed is over, they drop back into their positions, sitting, slouching, laying down, or sitting in their lawn chair just inches away from the bishop's chair.

Yes, it is theatrics and a mere curiosity for some, but the many stories I have heard since becoming bishop of this Diocese of Olympia, from young and old alike, make me ask, "So what?" It comes with humor too, which more of our practice should. Recently, some alums of the Compline Choir told about a Sunday evening in the 1960s when one of the choristers came running into the choir room to announce that a naked woman had crawled into the bishop's chair just before Compline was to begin. Another alum said, "Yes, and you never saw that choir room empty so quickly!"

Many of those attending Compline have been asked why they attend. There are as many responses as people, but an overwhelming consistency in the answers revolve around this general idea: "Here is a space like no other in my world. In my life I need *more*, and this gets me closer to that." They don't have to understand it. They simply feel it.

That reality, that need, and the change in generations are bumping up against a much more scientific and factual reality that, I believe, we are leaving behind (or at the very least putting in proper place and perspective). I am living in hope that we are coming to the realization that our traditions are not useless and dead, but rather mysterious and alluring to a new generation. It is not that our tradition is bad. The problem is that we don't know it anymore. It is more a lapse in formation than the need to leave it behind. It is also a bit of a misread about those who come to us searching.

I see this revealed in many ways. Some time ago, one of the rectors in our diocese contacted me about a request that had been made by a few in the church to stop reciting the Nicene Creed on Sunday. It turns out they no longer were sure if they believed it all. My first response was, "That is why we need to keep saying it every Sunday, because we are no longer sure we believe it all." But, after that, I also told him I would love to come and share with the congregation why I love it, why I do not want to lose it, and why I was saying no to their request.

I see it this way: The Creeds are the melody of Christianity. They are the song you cannot get out of your head. (I think this is why so many of the same people who would just as soon throw the Nicene Creed into the ditch of useless history sing hymns laced with some of the worst theology I can imagine with tears running down their faces.) Well taught and reflected upon, I think the Creeds can be that for us. They used to be chanted, not just said, singing of that which cannot be put fully into words.

Yes, I know, the Creeds are political documents, haggled over, and compromised. I get that totally. But I also believe in the power and cleverness of the Holy Spirit just enough to believe that grace can work through any process, and that it did in this one. These words are like the ancient tribal stories that elders and chiefs would tell. They would often end those with something like, "Now I don't know if it all happened just like that, but if you think about it long enough, you will know that it is true." I see the Creeds just the same way. They are words that attempt to describe the indescribable. It is our tune, our melody. We need to sing it, together, if for no other reason than to honor our ancestors who, in all their human frailty, desperately wanted to pass that melody down to future generations.

It is the difference between facts and truth. We have become a people of facts, and if no facts can be brought to bear on it, then it must not be true. The people that handed these Creeds down, along with our faith, were less interested in that version of the truth. We can make a leap—assuming we are smarter than they were—but I think we head down that road at our great peril. That is a road we have traveled of late, and it might be time for us to consider the next exit.

Many people are saying the Church is dying. I have never believed that. It is changing and always has been, but it is not dying. The Church belongs to God. It is the expression of God in this world. It will survive. The question is whether our form of honoring that tradition, our expression, our brand of it will survive. That, indeed, is up in the air, but that is also an entirely different question.

I have known Greg Garrett for over ten years, and in that time there is one thing I have never doubted about him: his belief that our church is not only alive, but is poised to change the world. He has never insinuated that the church is dying, nor does he carry himself like someone who thinks it is. He has lovingly challenged the church, to be sure, but more than anything he has helped me, and many I know and love, to see the church in a new light. In so doing he has revealed for us the church we know can be and is, if one only strives to see it.

In these past decades the Church has tried so many programs, strategies, and models. They can be effective, but the primary thing is knowing our motives, spending enough time digging ever deeper into our collective soul to see the sometimes rather self-centered nature of all of our effort to save the Church. It is not enough to know the "how" and the "what"; we have to also know the "why."

In my day-to-day vocation as bishop I am constantly amazed at some of the things on which we spend our energy and passion. I am equally convinced that when the church stays focused on sharing the message of Jesus Christ and on being that message in the world, then our motives are much closer to what the Church should and will be.

The question is this: Is anyone, inside or outside our ranks, being built up by our current witness? If not, I think we have to seriously consider whether or not we have ceased being the Church. That does not mean the Church has ceased to be, just that we have strayed from it. Having an address, keeping the lights on, doing what we have always done, is not a mission unless it points to, builds up, and nurtures a true deepening of the connection with our God.

I think there are two questions I am asked the most: "What is your favorite thing about being a bishop?" and "What makes you believe the Church is not dying?", and both can be answered in one story.

My favorite moment as bishop is the occasion when I lay hands on a person's head. In that moment I remember that I am, in this role, not only myself. In that moment I am reminded that the people gathered around me, including the one under my hand, are more than just individuals, more than simply a gathering of singularities. They are a community. They are one with those present, one with those who have gone before who participated in this same act, and one even with those who have not yet found this community in all the generations yet to come. In that moment, it has become my practice to leave a long silence. I explain to the confirmands beforehand that I leave that silence so that we are not rushed. But I also leave that silence so that I might pray for that person before I pray on behalf of the church, for all who have gone before them, and all that are yet to come, and I encourage those I bless to do the same.

I have never rushed, no matter how many confirmands I have had, and the service can get long. But I have been told over and over again by those under my hand and those who witness it that something profoundly moving happens in that silence. They are not alone. It never fails to happen for me too.

Several years ago one of those confirmands was a sixteen-year-old young woman. Throughout our meeting and our interaction beforehand, she seemed disconnected, oblivious, and uninterested. I tried to have a little fun with her and asked her if she ever smiled. She made sure she frowned as intentionally as she could. But in that moment of silence, with my hands on her head, with her family all around with their hands on her, with her church community surrounding her, and, I am convinced, with the awareness that the great cloud of witnesses and all of history was around her too, tears streamed down her face, and she smiled the biggest smile I had seen in a long while.

That is when I know as deeply as I can know anything: This church is not dying.

Such is my view and my hope.

This book, *My Church Is Not Dying*, is a revelation of Greg Garrett's blessed assurance of that hope. In the stories he tells and the people he shares, you too will, I believe, see a church fully alive.

The Right Reverend Greg Rickel, Bishop of Olympia

Introduction: My Church Is Not Dying

A century and a quarter ago, the great British historian Edward Gibbon wrote these words as he began to unfold one of the most radical changes in all of human history: "In the second century of the Christian era, the empire of Rome comprehended the fairest part of the earth, and the most civilized portion of mankind. The frontiers of that extensive monarchy were guarded by ancient renown and disciplined valour. The gentle, but powerful, influence of laws and manners had gradually cemented the union of the provinces. Their peaceful inhabitants enjoyed and abused the advantages of wealth and luxury."[1]

These are the first lines, as you may know, of Gibbon's *The Decline and Fall of the Roman Empire*, and they capture a great civilization at its exalted peak, just before its decline and disappearance. What he wrote about—that decline and fall—had jarred the world, not just the inhabitants of Rome, but all of those whose lives were touched by Rome. It is indeed a startling thing when great and powerful institutions shift or shrink. Often what we feel in these moments of radical change is confusion and anxiety. How did it happen? What are we supposed to do in this strange new world? Where (as The Kinks would sing) have all the good times gone?

The Romans are, of course, far from the only group to be on top of the world, to enjoy wealth and luxury—and then to see the earth shift underneath their feet. American Episcopalians, members of one of the

wealthiest and most influential churches in our country's history, likewise
find themselves in the place of having been at the pinnacle of modern life
and now being something else, possibly something less, definitely something different. One could—if one wished—even speak of something like
the Decline and Fall of the Episcopal Church. Certainly many people have,
and still do.

Here's a telling fact: If you Google "episcopal church decline," you'll
immediately (.22 seconds) call up 909,000 pertinent web pages. If, on
the other hand, you search for "episcopal church resurgence," you come
up with a tiny fraction of these results—many of which do not actually
seem to be about any resurgence of the Protestant Episcopal Church in
the United States of America, as the Episcopal Church officially is known.
And yet, I think these two searches are bound up together, and one of the
reasons this book needs to be written and read.

Yes, there are fewer Episcopalians than in the glory days of the
Church. Yes, times are changing, and the institution cannot go on being
the Church in the same way. And yes, strangely enough, I happen to get
up in the morning thinking that the Episcopal Church is filled with life
and light, and that it is and will continue to be a blessing to the world.

F. Scott Fitzgerald once remarked that to be able to simultaneously
hold two contradictory ideas in your mind was the mark of a superior
intellect. I'm going to ask you to demonstrate that trait as we explore both
the idea of what the Episcopal Church was and is no longer, and some
ideas about what it remains and may become. We are in a stretch of time
some people call the end, but my experience with and within the Church
suggests it is a new beginning. What the Church is going to be is being
defined right now by individual congregations across the US (and others in our tradition in England, Australia, Wales, France, and elsewhere
around the world), and by individuals who are both ordained people and
laypeople, bishops in purple, and barristas in Episcopal coffee shops.

I've seen much of this change at close range. I'll be talking in some
detail about churches in which I have served or been a parishioner, since
I've observed them closely and had the opportunity to see firsthand what
is working and what is not. In that sense, perhaps St. David's Episcopal
Church in Austin, Texas; Calvary Episcopal Church in Bastrop, Texas; and
St. James' Episcopal Church in Austin are over-represented (it was Henry

David Thoreau who explained in *Walden* that he was necessarily limited by his experience to writing about his own life), but I also think they represent positive examples of things happening all across the Episcopal world. I've also visited many other churches, and talked with many other Episcopalians and Anglicans who have shared their stories, their passions, and their dreams with me, and this book is the result of all those conversations, close by and far off.

Everyone who offered me their stories loves the Episcopal Church, loves their individual church, and sees an ongoing future for both, as do I. We may indeed be witnessing a crisis, but what I heard over and over from people in the research and writing of this book is that a crisis can actually be a good and necessary thing.

I have a coffee cup on my desk at Baylor University given to me by an ex-wife in a loving moment. It bears the Chinese ideogram, or *hanza*, for "crisis" on the front, and a short inspirational note on the back. John Kennedy, Condoleeza Rice, and Al Gore are just a few of the many people over the last sixty years who have also told my coffee cup's story that in Mandarin, the word for "crisis" is made up of the individual characters meaning "danger" and "opportunity." It turns out that this is not exactly true, but like Greg Rickel says of the Creeds in his foreword, many apocryphal stories, whether or not the facts fit, seem to be true in all the ways that count.

It's human nature that when we face danger, our fight or flight mechanisms go to work. Maybe we circle the wagons to fight off the opposing threat. Maybe we run for our lives, hoping to outdistance that threat. Maybe we pull the covers up over our heads and try to pretend we don't know about the threat; maybe if we don't see it, it won't see us!

But these moments of danger and potential destruction also offer clear opportunities for change, growth, and renewal. You probably know from your own life how difficult it is to make important, even necessary changes in the middle of day-to-day life. Often, it's not until things fall apart, in times when we must change or die, that we are able to do what we ought to have been doing long ago. And that seems to be the situation for the Episcopal Church as well. The crisis of the past decades became an opportunity to change, to grow, as well as to continue bringing the world some things it desperately needs.

Why change? Mostly because if we try to do business the way we always have, if we expect to survive just by opening our doors on Sunday morning and offering meaningful worship, we are done for. Beliefs have changed, our culture has changed, and the way that people relate to each other has changed.

What does it mean to be a church (or a Church) in the twenty-first century? That's the most meaningful question we can ask. How we respond to changing demographics, shifting views of faith and spirituality, and new ways of being community—while still remaining true to the mission of the Church—will dictate whether we indeed decline and fall, or whether we demonstrate a meaningful rebirth for however many people choose to be in some way a part of our journey.

My bishop, the Right Reverend Andrew Doyle, who serves the Diocese of Texas, says that the work of the Church is evangelism and mission. "Evangelism is sharing the Good News of Salvation through God in Christ Jesus with the world around us. Mission is doing that Gospel work through deeds. As Episcopalians we do both; it is not an either/or proposition. It is the very work of the Church to help people come to God."

If you accept this formulation of what the Episcopal Church is called to do—and as you'll see from this book, I do—the question shifts. How do we help people come to that awareness of God in a world where fewer people believe in God, fewer people attend formal church services, public respect for Christianity from non-Christians has plummeted, and people are simultaneously more connected and more alienated—from each other and from themselves—than at any time in history?

Beliefs have changed. Our culture has changed. Let's chart the extent of those changes by observing the height that a modern-day Gibbon might cite for the Episcopal Church before the supposed decline and fall. In the post-WWII years in America, it was widely expected that (if you weren't Jewish!) you would be in church on Sunday. In those days in a much smaller America, about three and a half million people called themselves Episcopalians. Today, the number is less than two million. Over the past fifty years, the Episcopal Church has clearly suffered a precipitous drop in attendance, as have other so-called "mainline" churches, including the United Methodist Church, Evangelical Lutheran Church in America (ELCA), Presbyterian Church (USA), and the Church of Christ.

This decline in attendance has led some (often people who are hoping for just this outcome), to extrapolate our slow but inevitable death.

Me? I laugh whenever someone tells me that the Episcopal Church is dying, because that phrase seems so at odds with my experience of both myself and of the Church. I actually first ended up attending the Episcopal Church in the early 2000s, in the midst of the cultural struggles we'll discuss in a later chapter.

I didn't know about these battles until later, and I didn't care. I came to church because I was dying. Literally. Chronic, serious depression, which had been sapping my strength since I was a teenager, had taken me over like a cancer. I was dying slowly at that precise moment, but I had experienced some narrow escapes, and I knew that if left to my own spiritual and emotional resources, I was likely to step off the planet in a big hurry sometime soon.

It was in the midst of my own turmoil that I walked in the door of St. James' Episcopal Church in Austin, Texas. I had never been in an Episcopal Church, but a long and mostly unaccountable set of coincidences had put it on my radar and something—somebody—had told me that I needed to go there. So I walked in the door, took a seat in the last row, and I sat and shivered while people tried to make me feel at home.

It was on that first Sunday morning at St. James' that I heard the Reverend Greg Rickel (now the Right Reverend Greg Rickel) pronounce from behind the altar the words that may have saved my life: "Wherever you are in your walk of faith, you are welcome at this table."

As I said, I didn't know then about the local, regional, and national fights over women's ordination and human sexuality that were sending many Episcopalians out of their churches and out of the denomination. I didn't know that most American denominations were in decline, with the so-called mainline denominations among the most deeply wounded. I didn't even know about the hordes of Americans leaving Christian faith altogether (the so-called "Nones," for "None of the Above") because of their negative perceptions about how Christianity was being lived out in the public square, or their perception that Christianity was somehow irrelevant to their lives.

All that is to say, when I walked into St. James', I didn't know I was coming into what many were calling a dying Church. I just knew that I was dying—and if I couldn't find life in this place, I couldn't find it anywhere. I don't suppose there's much suspense about what happened next—I mean, I am writing these words in 2014, over a decade later. I survived. No, more than that; I thrived. I was brought back to life, set on my feet again, offered hope and community, and surrounded by beauty and by understandings of the world, of God, and of myself that made sense to me.

Simply put: I am alive today because I was rescued by one particular Episcopal church in East Austin, a community that manifested hospitality, compassion, and social justice as the expressions of its faith. I became an Episcopalian officially because I discovered it to be a welcoming tradition that valued art, beauty, intellect, questions, and service to others. After my rescue, I was encouraged by my church to attend the Episcopal seminary in Austin (which I did full-time for three years, earning my Master of Divinity degree), and I even offered myself for the Episcopal priesthood at a time when some people told me there might not be an Episcopal Church when I graduated from seminary.

The Church and I agreed ultimately that ordination for parish ministry was not going to be my path, but I continue today to serve as an Episcopal preacher, teacher, retreat leader, and theologian because I have found a home in the Episcopal Church, because for me it is the very best place to try to be a faithful person, even in a world that is rapidly leaving Christian faith behind.

We talked earlier about danger and opportunity. I can tell you from experience that facing death makes you realize things. You realize that you can't go on the way you have been. You realize that if you're going to continue living, you've got to reclaim or foreground the things that make existence worthwhile.

I found that true in my own life, and I think those truths apply to the Episcopal Church as well. We have been, for some time, taking stock, but eventually, if we're going to go on, we have to pull the trigger on some big decisions stemming from those big questions:

What does it mean to be Episcopalian in the twenty-first century?

What does the Episcopal Church stand for in an age when people continue to claim our church—and maybe all Christian churches—are dying?

Why would anybody want to become—or remain—Episcopalian in this environment?

Why are some Episcopal churches (including the one I currently serve, St. David's Episcopal Church in Austin, Texas) and some dioceses adding members even in the midst of all these doubts and questions?

What does the Episcopal Church have to offer a broken world—and how can we make the world aware of those gifts?

This is a book that seeks to wrestle with those questions and to suggest some helpful and hopeful answers. It is a book for practicing Episcopalians and Anglicans who might wonder what our tradition still has to offer an increasingly complex and secular world, and for Episcopal church leaders (lay and ordained) who want to remind themselves or discover anew the treasures and possibilities open to those of us who claim descent from the Church of England but who live out our lives in these United States.

It is a book that takes seriously both my experience as Professional Church Person (seminarian, preacher, lecturer, consultant) and as a Person in a Pew (which is where I spend most Sundays, with my family).

It is a book that supplements my personal experience of the Church across the country and around the world with the stories, dreams, and hopes of leaders and worshippers, from the Most Reverend Katharine Jefferts Schori, presiding bishop of the Episcopal Church USA, and the Most Reverend Rowan Williams, past archbishop of Canterbury, to people in the pews, and even to some outside the walls of the Church. These many thoughts about what it means to be Episcopalian today are a vital part of the book, for those I quote offer new and real insights into how God might be moving in the world and how we might respond to that movement. These hundreds of suggestions, questions, and affirmations from across the Church make this book far more valuable than if I were only offering my own suggestions, questions, and affirmations.

It is a book that asks who we are today, who we might be tomorrow, and how we might get from one place to the other. As Tom Brackett, a consultant for the national church, asks, how can we "molt out of the old shells that once defined and now inhibit us"?[2]

It's also a book that suggests that maybe many of us are already doing that, stepping out of some of our old clothes that don't fit so well anymore, while holding onto those fashions that will never go out of style.

All of those things are about our present and our future. But to see who we are and where we might be going, it's also necessary to take a step back and reflect on our past. Episcopalians have always been a small group—in America we now represent less than 1 percent of the population—and if people know about us, chances are they don't always know us very well. They may not know where we came from, what we stand for, or who we are. As Bishop Wayne Wright of Delaware told me, Episcopalians spend too much time trying to explain what we aren't, and not enough celebrating what we are.

My Grandma Irene—admittedly from a small town in Oklahoma without an Episcopalian near—asked me after I was confirmed into St. James' if "Episcopals believe in Jesus." She honestly didn't know. And my guess is that plenty of others don't know about us, because I didn't know about us either, and I had gotten thousands and thousands of miles away from that small town in Oklahoma. Before I became an Episcopalian, what I thought I knew was that Episcopalians drank and played golf. It's a misunderstanding just true enough to be funny, but hardly a rounded portrait of our denomination and its adherents.

Even when people do know something about Episcopal and Anglican Christians, their perceptions may be skewed by our past, or by those recent headlines about our faith that don't capture the whole picture—by our past battles over gay bishops, or about homosexual blessing, or legal wrangling over church property. So another of the tasks of this book is to pause for a moment and fill in the details, both for people coming to the tradition anew and for those of us who fill the pews some Sunday mornings or serve the homeless some Sunday afternoons. Not all of us know where we came from either.

"How did we get here?" is always a seminal question. As novelist William Faulkner—himself a sometime adherent who lies buried in the churchyard of St. Peter's Episcopal Church in Oxford, Mississippi—used to say, "The past isn't dead. It isn't even past."

Whatever people think they know about the Episcopal Church shapes their reaction to it—and their participation in it. So here in the Introduction, let's take a moment to explore where we came from, who we've been, and where we seem to many to be going. In the process, we'll refute some simple misunderstandings, acknowledge some past failings, and, in the process, pick up some wisdom for the journey.

How did we get here? Like this:

It's true. We are at least partly the product of a disagreement about divorce between the pope of the Roman Catholic Church and England's King Henry VIII, once a young lion who fought for the purity of the Catholic faith, later a rotund serial monogamist seeking the Church's legitimization of a wife—any wife!—who would bear him a male heir. Visitors touring the apartments of Henry's Hampton Court Palace today can hear a ghost (okay, more probably a tape loop) whispering the spooky and disgusting litany of the Six Wives of Henry the Eighth: "Divorced. Beheaded. Died. Divorced. Beheaded. Survived."

That roll call of selfish ambition doesn't seem a propitious way to start any great endeavor, maybe most especially a Church. The whole business seems more than a little sordid, and also more than a little mercenary. The king's later grab for the incredible wealth and land controlled by the Roman Church and its monastic establishments wouldn't reflect well on anyone, and represents one of the worst acts of religious vandalism in all of history.

But Henry's divorce is only a part of our story, the presenting issue. We are also the product of decades of struggle involving faithful scholars, priests, kings and queens, who sought an authentic way of being the catholic body of Christ in England—and heirs of the centuries of British and Celtic Christianity that predated Henry's disputes with Rome.

From the soap-opera headlines, the martyrdoms and executions and hypocrisy and apostasy, we gained an understanding that Christianity has to be about something other than what we say we believe or what political party we favor. Those determinants only lead us into conflict, not concord, and so a vital part of the Anglican endeavor became the attempt to find a way for Christians to get along—and stay together—that revolved around more than accepted dogma. In later chapters, we'll explore how this hard-won wisdom that emerged from bloody British history still informs Episcopal ways of worship, community, and hospitality, and could be a vital offering we make to a world filled with conflict and division.

Despite the violence and discord we associate with the founding of the Church of England, something beautiful emerged. Set aside portly King Henry for a moment; we are also partly the brilliant idea of Thomas Cranmer, a scholar whom Henry made the archbishop of Canterbury, the leader of the Church of England.

The king wanted Cranmer to engineer his divorce from his wife of eighteen years, Catherine of Aragon, but the archbishop proved to be much more than a reliable religious flunky. Cranmer understood that an English Church needed an English way of worship and a distinctly English way of prayer, and so he reworked traditional Latin prayers drawn from a liturgy that the English Catholic Church had used for centuries (the Sarum Missal, employed at Salisbury Cathedral) into an English prayer book that anyone could employ in daily worship.

Cranmer's Book of Common Prayer went through several revisions as succeeding generations fought about how Catholic or Puritan it should or shouldn't be, but that idea of daily prayer for all is the particular genius of the Anglican tradition, handed down from Cranmer directly to us. "These daily offices derive from the monastic orders when people withdrew to commune with God," says the Reverend Canon Liz Hendrick, who serves at the American Cathedral in Paris. "Their goal was to draw closer to God, so they removed all distractions."[3] From the monastic tradition of hourly prayer, Cranmer distilled morning, noon, and evening prayers, making it possible for people who had jobs or children to nonetheless be involved in a daily life of the Spirit. For the first time, one didn't have to be a monastic to live a life of prayer.

What the Reverend Mary Earle, a retired priest and writer from San Antonio, says she loves most about the Anglican tradition is "everyday practice," and in the prayers, or in the saying of the Daily Office from the prayer book, Episcopalians can find themselves drawn into prayer alongside millions of other Anglicans around the globe.

For well over 450 years, some version of the prayer book has marked the hours for us (the 1662 edition continues to be in use in England 350 years later), and done so with language and metaphor that have become familiar to most people, even if they don't know their origin. Cranmer perhaps did not know that he was writing and compiling one of the most enduring works of English literature in addition to creating a functional prayer book, but if the gifts of the Anglican tradition had stopped with the Book of Common Prayer, they would still be worth celebrating.

Literary critics like my Baylor colleague Alan Jacobs have written about its beauty and influence, both of which are immense. As James Woods, who wrote an introduction for Penguin's edition of the Book of

Common Prayer, observed in *The New Yorker*, "the acute poetry, balanced sonorities, heavy order, and direct intimacy of Cranmer's prose have achieved permanence, and many of his phrases and sentences are as famous as lines from Shakespeare or the King James Bible."[4] Some scholars in fact opine that the English language has been metaphorically frozen in place over the past five hundred years by the concurrent greatness of Shakespeare, the King James Bible, and the Book of Common Prayer. Just compare our ability to read their English and Geoffrey Chaucer's English; Chaucer was writing only two hundred years before Shakespeare, but his Middle English is impenetrable to us today. Most of Shakespeare, the Bible, and the Prayer Book, however, read to us like modern English. With a few archaic exceptions, we understand it well, and are often moved by the beauty of its expression and the richness of its language.

People who have never opened the prayer book know the phrases "Earth to earth, ashes to ashes, dust to dust" from the burial service, or "to have and to hold from this day forward, for better for worse, for richer for poorer, in sickness and in health, to love and to cherish, till death do us part." Cranmer's words and rhythms have become part of us like a much-loved song or a famous speech. Even non-Episcopalians are a tiny bit Episcopalian because of it. We'll return to the prayer book—which remains the defining element for Anglicans and Episcopalians—in our chapters on the Anglican way, worship, beauty, and justice. It's that important, and it cuts across almost all of the facets of Anglican and Episcopal life.

Besides Cranmer's prayer book, Henry's desire for a truly English church, and generations of debate and struggle to worship together, we are also partly the brilliant idea of an American elite: the wealthy planters, the bankers, the purveyors of culture, the Founding Fathers. For centuries, in any town where we had a church presence we were a power to be reckoned with, and while we were always small in numbers, the Episcopal Church exerted an outsized influence. Over half of those who signed our nation's formational documents were Episcopalians. Since then, eleven United States presidents (most recently Gerald Ford and the first President Bush; George W. Bush was raised Episcopal but it didn't stick), over 30 percent of all Supreme Court justices (Sandra Day O'Connor and David Souter among them), an inordinate number of people in Congress (including Senator Kay Bailey Hutchison from Texas, Senator John McCain from

Arizona, and the retired senator from Missouri, John Danforth, who is an Episcopal priest), and plenty of other luminaries have been Episcopalians. Because of this history and these connections, Episcopalians have exerted more influence on our politics and culture than any other similarly sized group (with the possible exception of American Jews, who actually out-number us).

We should acknowledge the obvious corollary truth—that members of the Episcopal Church boast among the highest per capita incomes of those in any faith group. That's why the stereotypes of limousine rides and martinis on yachts—not to mention my golf-playing, single-malt-drinking Episcopalian—emerge. Some Episcopalians are wealthy and powerful. Plenty of us, of course, are not. I do not own a mansion; I do not drive a Cadillac or ride in a limo; my parents are neither wealthy nor from distinguished families; my kids are not in exclusive private schools; I don't get my picture in the society pages just for showing up. Like many others, I am an Episcopalian not because I was born into it, but because I chose it, and I chose it for reasons having nothing to do with wealth and power—mine or the Church's.

But our presence in the halls of power has shaped us in positive ways as well as some obvious negatives. The democratic polity of our national church—an assembly with an upper and lower house—is based on the United States Constitution, which many Episcopalians read and signed in its original form. Like the United States, our leaders, including our national leader, the presiding bishop of the Episcopal Church, are elected (not, say, chosen by a committee and later confirmed by the queen, as is the archbishop of Canterbury). The bishop who will replace our current presiding bishop, the Most Reverend Katharine Jefferts Schiori—the first female primate or head of a national church in the Anglican world—will be elected by a vote of the next General Assembly at the 2015 Episcopal General Convention.

Episcopalians—while we are certainly not perfect at tolerance and welcome—can model a democratic melting pot of diverse cultures, beliefs, social classes, and political parties as we come together in common wor-ship. St. James', Austin, was one of the first truly multicultural institutions I had ever seen. That historically African American church had opened its doors to gay and lesbian people, to mixed-race couples, to people from

Africa and Asia, and even to depressed white straight males like me, and it celebrated all of us as essential parts of the body of Christ. As the Reverend Mary Certain Vano, a priest from Arkansas, points out, at our best the Episcopal Church can model "an open-minded faith that places our love for Christ and one another above like-mindedness." Austin layperson Diane Owens seconds those thoughts: "The Church embraces different cultures, different views, and different values." In our chapters on community, the culture wars, and reaching out to others, we'll explore how our desire to be a diverse community mirrors America's story, and how we can help remind our culture what is best about the American dream.

A part of our story is about failure and fracture. As I mentioned earlier, headlines in both secular and religious media sound the death knells of the Episcopal Church (and practically every other church): Millennials are leaving the Church! Boomer believers are dying like flies! The "Nones" (the religiously unaffiliated, or None of the Above) are the fastest growing demographic in America! A Baptist minister actually asked me recently if I thought the Episcopal Church was going to survive, and my first answer was, "I think everybody who was going to leave has already left." Then I stopped, reflected, and offered a more useful answer: "Of course the Episcopal Church is going to survive. But it's going to be different."

It's going to survive. But it's going to be different. That response could be applied to almost all of the Protestant mainline denominations. All of us have trimmed budgets and reevaluated assets and operations. We have all had to trim or sell off subsidiary ministries—church conference centers, publishing houses, real estate. Whatever the mainline denominations look like going forward, they will look very little like the towering powers of the mid-twentieth century.

The days when Episcopalians (and other denominations) could assume that if they simply opened the doors of their churches, people were culturally conditioned to attend are over. But our contention with decline—and our contention with the persistent conflicts that have in some cases worsened the exodus from our denomination—have had their bright sides as well. We've learned that we have to be about something more than open doors—and we've had to wrestle with what it means to call something "church." We'll discuss that in our chapters on worship and community.

But this too is true: Some of us have actually been brought *into* the Church by the tolerance and progressive theology that led to our great conflicts. I know this for a fact, since I am one of them. After years of scorning Christian involvement, I chose to be formally affiliated with the Episcopal Church *because* of its loving stance toward gay and lesbian Christians and its embrace of women as full partners in the sacramental life of the Church.

Jason van Borssum, a postulant for holy orders in the Diocese of Los Angeles, argues that the Episcopal Church has actually benefited from the hard experience of the last decades, even though it cost us members, because it has put us in a better place to address the post-Christian culture that America is becoming. Because we've already dealt with issues other churches are still trying to navigate, he suggests, we can be authentically welcoming to generations who feel put off by years of Christian moralizing and infighting, and can welcome everyone we encounter, without fear of further division in our churches.

This goes for gays and lesbians in the pews and in ministry; it also goes for women. Lory Hunt, minister of youth at an Episcopal church in Paris, Texas, went to a Baptist seminary. After graduation, she found ministry prospects limited in her own denomination. Many churches were still unready to employ a female pastor, still unsure about putting a woman in the pulpit. When I asked the Facebook world one morning what they were celebrating about the Episcopal Church, Lory's response was short and heartfelt: "I love that I can pursue my full and true calling, not having to settle for something less than I've been called to do and be." On the far end of the culture wars, as we will see in our chapter called "Living Together," is a place where we are more ready, perhaps than any other group of contemporary Christians, to reach out to today's world.

The agreement of those of us who have made it through the Episcopal Wars is very simple: We are still here, together, on a journey toward God, and it isn't so much about being right or wrong as it is being here, together. We're all searching for answers—but are suspicious of anyone who feels she or he *has* all the answers. The Reverend Erin Jean Warde, who serves as college chaplain to Baylor University, puts it beautifully: "I'm an Episcopalian because the Episcopal Church is about discernment over dogma. The primary punctuation of the Episcopal Church is a question mark, not a period." And Marcy McKay, a lay leader in Amarillo, Texas, seconds the sentiment: "I love the Episcopal Church because I do *not* have to check my brain at the door."

Our willingness to live into a life of community oriented toward God, our willingness to welcome a diverse group of others to share our journey, our willingness to live out the questions in our daily lives in the world are all part of what it means to be Episcopalians. We'll consider these in detail in the chapters on living the questions, living together, touching other lives, and telling the world about our faith.

So yes, we are the Church of schism and controversy, but we are also the Church of welcome and acceptance. We are the Church of power and privilege, but we are also the Church of racial and economic justice. We are the Church of the frozen chosen, but we are also a Church who loves beauty and feels deeply. We have been a Church that ostracizes, but we can also be the Church that reconciles.

We have deserved many of the bad things that people have believed about us—and we have manifested so many good things that people don't even know about.

So here is the truth about the Anglican/Episcopal tradition, and why some of us have given our lives to worshipping and serving within it: Granting every perceived—or actual—negative about who we are, where we came from, or what we are at our worst, at our best we are something equally powerful, totally positive, and absolutely worth sharing with the world. The Reverend Stephen Kidd, who ministers in Gulfport, Mississippi, brings many of the strains of this opening meditation together when he reflects on why he is an Episcopalian:

> The Episcopal Church welcomed me when others wouldn't have me, and honored my questions when others simply sought to dismiss them. Its sacramental life spoke to parts of my soul that the fundamentalism of my childhood couldn't touch; worship felt ancient, holy, and real in ways I didn't expect. Fifteen years later I am still amazed at the depth and breadth of our tradition, and I appreciate all the more our peculiar vantage point at the intersection of the Protestant, Catholic and Orthodox corners of our Christian family. The Episcopal Church isn't perfect, far from it, but for me, it is home.

The Episcopal Church is a place where you can participate in Evensong, a sung version of the evening prayer service in which Christians have been participating since the second century—and an event that may induce you to tweet, pin photos, or Facebook it so that the world can know what a powerfully transformative experience you find it.

The Episcopal Church is a place where every Sunday, priests recite liturgy that Christians have been repeating for the last two thousand years, and, in their sermons, they may discuss hip-hop, commercials, sporting events, and the news of the moment.

The Episcopal Church is a place where every Sunday we eat the bread and drink the wine in memory of Jesus—but every week we are reminded in our liturgies that communion is intended to fuel us to live out Jesus' mission in our own world in the coming week.

The Episcopal Church is a place where day in and day out, priests and parishioners reach out to each other as members of a loving community—and day in and day out, they reach out to the world in love and service, building homes, feeding the hungry, and serving those who suffer because that is what we are called to do.

The Episcopal Church is changing, and it is life-changing. It is made up of saints and of imperfect people like myself. And for me, as for Stephen, Erin, Tom, Jason, Mary, Greg, Marcy, Andy, Diane, Lory, and so many more of us—the Episcopal Church is our home.

If you want to experience life in abundance—and express to others how and where they might find it—then I invite you to follow me deeper into conversation. Perhaps, as Jesus says, Our Father's House does have many mansions, but for me and over a million other saints, this is our dwelling place. And maybe you will discover that you, too, could make our house a home. If the Episcopal Church is your home, if you would like to think that it could be, or if you would like to imagine how any faith tradition could be, I would love to be your guide as together we explore the Episcopal Church of the twenty-first century, a place of ancient wisdom and modern practice.

Questions for Discussion

1. What draws you to read this book? What is your own history of engagement with the Episcopal tradition?
2. What does it mean to say a tradition is in decline? Is size the only meaningful metric for a church or denomination, or do other elements factor into such a measurement?
3. How do you think churches need to change to engage an increasingly secular culture? What practices of your own church (or of churches you have observed) seem to be reaching people?
4. What do you think about the idea that Americans in general are less drawn to communal activities? Have you seen evidence of that in your own life? What would it take to draw you into a group or new community?

For Further Reading

John R. H. Moorman, *History of the Church in England* (New York: Church Publishing, 1980).

Moorman was an English scholar who also served as an Anglican priest and bishop, and his classic history of Christianity in England from the Romans to the late twentieth century has substantial sections on the English Reformation and the creation and growing pains of the Church of England.

Phyllis Tickle, *The Great Emergence: How Christianity Is Changing and Why* (Grand Rapids, MI: Baker Books, 2012).

Tickle, an Episcopal laywoman who served as the first religion editor for *Publishers Weekly*, draws from her years of reading and her wide observation to discuss the massive five-hundred-year shift she sees happening in Christianity, and to assess the dangers and opportunities awaiting the Church in the twenty-first century.

Christopher Webber, *Welcome to the Episcopal Church: An Introduction to Its History, Faith, and Worship* (New York: Morehouse, 1999).

A priest and writer, Webber offers this accessible introduction to the Episcopal Church, briefly but thoughtfully laying out our history, liturgy, and beliefs, and offering readers questions for discussion and further thought.

The Anglican Way: Spiritual and Religious

It is evening, and the shadows are falling fast. Outside the church it may already be dark; inside we sit in candlelight. "Oh God, make speed to save us," a lone voice chants, and others join in, their notes echoing in the great open space, "Oh Lord, make haste to help us."

It could be Sunday night in my home parish in Austin, St. David's, where the choir is singing a prayer service called Compline. It could be any evening at the National Cathedral, in Washington, DC, when choral Evensong is being offered to God. It could be late afternoon in Canterbury Cathedral, Westminster Abbey, St. Paul's in London, or one of the college chapels at Cambridge or Oxford. Wherever you are, sung evening prayer is one of the most beautiful and distinctive elements of Anglican faith and practice. Since the Book of Common Prayer was first released in 1549, choirs in England and the rest of the Anglican world have sung a moving service of prayer and thanksgiving at day's end.

It's a service that was created during times of great uncertainty and turmoil—we still use prayers that ask God to protect us through the night—and this great gift of Anglican worship continues to speak to us in our own uncertainty and turmoil.

Episcopalians are Anglican—that is, they are part of the Anglican Communion, a worldwide gathering of national churches under the leadership of the Church of England and the archbishop of Canterbury. The Communion is a confederation, not a top-down structure (as past archbishops of Canterbury have learned to their dismay), and the various members of the Communion around the world vary widely in their stances on social, cultural, and theological questions. If you were to ask members of the Anglican Church in Canada and of the Church of Nigeria (who might tell you they no longer consider themselves part of the Anglican Communion) how they feel about women in ministry or about gays in the Church, you are liable to get deeply contradictory answers.

But whatever we may believe about liturgy or gay marriage or feeding the poor or proper church music, we all have one thing in common: We all partake of the prayer book tradition that sprouts from Cranmer's original Book of Common Prayer.

It's important to be reminded that we are part of something bigger than ourselves with the prayer book at its heart. Americans in particular place a great value on rugged individualism, and we are prone to take our ball and go home when we don't like the way the game is going. Phyllis Tickle, a writer and Episcopal lay leader from Tennessee, often says that the IRS recognizes over twenty thousand Protestant denominations—each of them the result of a group of churchgoers taking their ball and going home. But, despite our own examples of priests, parishes, and even the occasional whole diocese trying to flee the denomination, Episcopalians are part of a tradition that calls us to play together—and if possible to play nice—because when we do, something truly beautiful happens.

The Reverend David Sugeno (who serves a parish in the Texas Hill Country) and I used to play guitar together in seminary. Together with the Reverend Cathy Boyd, who serves alongside David in Marble Falls, we would lead worship or play concerts or entertain at parties or just sit down to jam together. Although we favored somewhat different kinds of music, we chose to play together. When we sang together, we gave up our solo careers singing lead and allowed ourselves to create a wondrous harmony of voices and chords you can only get when you have spent time playing with somebody and have learned to trust and maybe even to love them. I still remember that what emerged from our time playing together was the kind of music you can only make when you feel secure enough to be yourself, the kind of music you can only make when you trust your fellow singers, the kind of music that only emerges out of true community.

That's why I thought it somehow appropriate that it was Dave Sugeno who asked me a formative question after I was first asked to write this book: "Why is it important that we come from an English tradition?"

Immediately I thought about the rugged individualism I mentioned above. Americans are solo artists; our heroes are lone wolves. Rambo and Batman are two of our archetypal American heroes, and they represent our belief that a single person who tries hard enough can succeed at anything. But when you look at English stories—think about the epic adventures of Harry Potter, Ron Weasley, and Hermione Granger, or the cases of Sherlock Holmes and Dr. Watson—they suggest a different way of seeing the world, in which we need each other to thrive and survive, in which we are all a part of something rather than exceptions to it. If our great novels are about singular individuals who are trying to become who they want to be (as in *Huck Finn* or *The Great Gatsby*), British literature and culture tends to ask how human beings fit into society rather than how they can be outside of it, unchained from it. It's a wholly different way of seeing ourselves and the world.

In this respect, Dave's question suggests that there might be a number of fruitful reasons it is important that we come from an English tradition, the first of which must be that it reminds us that we are meant to be part of a larger whole. American religion too often emphasizes individual belief and religious experience; some of our Christian brothers and sisters, for example, foreground the importance of taking Jesus as one's "personal lord and savior," of having what they call a personal relationship with Jesus Christ.

Some American Christians flit from church to church seeking the one place that will perfectly match them and their beliefs. Other Americans treat faith and spirituality as a smorgasbord from which they can take a little Buddhist mindfulness, a sprinkle of Islamic charity, a pinch of Benedictine order, and roll it all into wisdom they use for their own personal advancement. Church or religious institutions may simply be means to the end of individual salvation or enlightenment.

The Anglican tradition stands in contrast to the purely personal spirituality practiced by many Americans. Our tradition is broad, and it encompasses many practices and beliefs, but it also still suggests that the heart of human spirituality is not personal advancement but common praise, that we are saved not in our own bodies, but in corporate bodies. Bishop Andy Doyle notes that as Episcopalians, "we believe that it is in Christian fellowship that we come to know Jesus in the power of the Holy Spirit, and that such stories are translated and interpreted through the eyes of worship and scripture . . . through fellowship, we discover our salvation."

The importance of community—that we are saved by and for each other, not by and for ourselves—is an ancient idea. St. Anthony the Great, the founder of desert monasticism, was surrounded by hermits who had fled civilization to seek enlightenment, but he knew that even for such radical individualists as the Desert Fathers and Mothers, "Our life and our death is with our neighbor. If we gain our brother, we have gained God, but if we scandalize our brother, we have sinned against Christ."[5] That lesson is approaching two thousand years old, and many American Christians still have not learned it. But for those of us who descend from the Church of England, reminders appear daily in our liturgy, in our diversity, and in our commitment to common prayer.

Presiding Bishop Katharine Jefferts Schori told me that this recentering is the very DNA of the Episcopal Church: "We encourage people to love God and God's creation (human and otherwise) with the same attention and passion with which we love ourselves. It's about learning that none of us as individuals occupy the center of the universe, and that a holy and whole and healed life seeks the flourishing and well-being of the rest, not ourselves alone."

This is certainly a countercultural way of being; individual Americans (me included) probably need to be reminded on a daily basis that they are not the center of the universe. But a tradition that incorporates community, and that suggests that I am at my best when I am shaped, challenged, and supported by my brothers and sisters, does remind me on a daily basis what truly matters. That is a gift from our English tradition—and from the overarching idea of the Anglican Communion.

The name of our church—the Protestant Episcopal Church in the United States of America—reflects a simultaneous break from and embrace of the traditions we inherited from the Church of England. Once we launched a Revolution against England (you may have heard about it), we could no longer recite the prayers for the British royal family in the liturgy, yet the words on either side of those prayers still spoke to our hearts and our situations. American Episcopalians were no longer a part of the Church of England after the Revolutionary War, but they still believed in governance by elected bishops, in organization by dioceses and parishes, and in democratic meetings where they voted to determine important policies.

They still worshipped in parishes distributed in small geographical regions more like neighborhoods than today's city-wide churches. They still thought the spiritual leadership of priests and deacons ordained by bishops (who had themselves been ordained by bishops who had been ordained by bishops, a principle known in the Catholic traditions as "apostolic succession") was a powerful model for spiritual leadership that also conferred a sense of historic connection to the larger Christian tradition.

And, of course, they accepted that a Book of Common Prayer—an American version—would be the basis for their worship together, whether they were Southern planters, Northern whalers, or Northwestern fur traders.

Despite our rejection of some of the worship language of the Church of England, we remain much more like the CoE than we have become unlike it, and so it's essential that we grasp how this tradition has shaped twenty-first century Episcopalians. Christianity in England was indeed shaped by the sixteenth-century split with the Roman Catholic Church, but that history stretches back much further than Henry VIII. It goes back to Roman Britain, and also includes a similar but distinctive tradition of Celtic Christianity that had been largely lost but has been reclaimed in the last two centuries.

Christianity originally came to Britain from two directions. The official mission of Augustine of Canterbury (not to be confused with the much better known Augustine of Hippo) came to the British Isles in 597. Augustine was the first archbishop of Canterbury, and one of the formal founders of the English Church. But there was another Christianity already in place, the indigenous Christianity represented by St. Patrick (fifth century CE), St. Columba (sixth century CE), and the great monasteries of Iona (563 CE) and Lindisfarne (635 CE), which were founded by Irish missionaries.

It's probably too reductive to simply place this native Christianity in opposition to Roman Catholic Christianity. The traditions employed different practices to set the date of Easter and its monks cut their hair differently, although both groups would have identified themselves as followers of Christ who accepted the authority of the Pope in far-off Rome. But it's easy to find both superficial and substantial differences. Celtic Christians often understood God to be moving in all of life, not just inside the church during the service of prayer or Eucharist. They encountered God in nature, on journeys, and in beautiful things, and the tradition of which we are a part still claims this deeply incarnational spirituality, a faith that God is moving in the world and present for us to claim, if we have eyes to see and ears to hear.

This Celtic spirituality was also deeply embedded in the everyday lives of the people who practiced it. Scholars starting in the nineteenth century began to recover prayers that had been a part of this native Christianity for centuries, and these prayers from Ireland, Scotland, Wales, and England often have a homely quality because they are about the most mundane of practices. Celtic Christians composed prayers to be recited when lighting the morning fire and banking the evening fire. They composed prayers for weaving, and prayers for turning the cows out to pasture. They prayed that the angels would be present as they worked and as they slept. Nothing in human life was considered to be too insignificant to involve in prayer.

An old Celtic saying, "Heaven is six feet above a person's head," acknowledges that we are not so far removed from the next world as we sometimes imagine, and that God is not some distant deity sitting on a throne somewhere. Many of the prayers and songs and pieces of liturgy that have grown out of this tradition imagine God as near at all times, imagine Christ accompanying us on our daily journeys, and suggest the great crowd of witnesses swirling about us, saints and angels close at hand.

During the morning Eucharist at Gladstone's Library in Hawarden, Wales, the Reverend Peter Francis closes the Prayers of the People by invoking "Christ, our brother and companion on the way." It is a distillation of this Celtic belief that faith is not segmented from our lives—something to be experienced only on Sunday morning, say—but interwoven with our lives. What this liturgy suggests, in fact, is that the daily practice of our faith *is* our real life, and that Jesus walks with us every step of the way.

The prayer book tradition also partakes of this awareness that faith is what goes on every day, and that we are not seeking a destination so much as we are people on a daily journey. Mary Earle's love for the everyday spirituality of the Episcopal Church reminds us that the Book of Common Prayer offers us a framework for regular encounters with God, all in concert with the believers praying around the world. At this—or any— moment, I could stop what I'm doing (that is, writing this sentence), pick up the Book of Common Prayer (or call it up on my computer, or even an app on my phone), and turn my thoughts to morning, noon, or evening prayer. I could read the lessons of the Daily Office (a daily lectionary used by many of my priest friends). I could recite a creed that's been in use for centuries as a way of reminding myself about the essentials of what I believe and hear in its familiar words God moving again in my life.

None of these words belong to me—that is, they are not the extemporaneous products of my heart—and yet they are my own. Repeated day by day, year by year, the liturgy of the prayer book has become like my blood and bones, below my surface yet necessary so that I can walk through my days. Sometimes I hardly notice it's there. Sometimes it shakes me to my very foundation. I am a different person every time I read, hear, or recite it, and so like any great and powerful work, it affects me differently day by day, year by year.

In our experience of the language of the prayer book—whether the seventeenth-century prayer book still in use in English churches or the 1979 prayer book employed in American churches—we are also partaking in some of the most beautiful language available to us, another tangible gift from the Anglican tradition. As we saw in the Introduction, Thomas Cranmer's prayer book launched phrases that have become a part of our common tongue: "movable feast" and "vile body," "miserable sinners" and "peace in our time." Thanks to its beauty, dignity, and majesty, we participate in beautiful worship by saying words that are not are own but that we have come to own: "Lord, open our lips / And our mouth shall proclaim your praise."

Different Anglican Churches around the globe have created different versions of the prayer book—the liturgies of the Welsh and New Zealand prayer books seem particularly lovely to many American churches, who incorporate them in their own worship—but all of them operate for the faithful in the same way: They present the opportunity for daily worship in a country's vernacular English, in communion with others, or in prayer with the rest of the body of Christ even when we are alone.

They offer us beautiful liturgy for the Eucharist, laments when we have no words of our own, and services to mark the great sacramental moments of our lives: baptism, marriage, confession, dying, and death. The prayer book gives us resources for both the monumental challenges of our lives and for the everyday. In it, theological belief finds its manifestation in daily practice. In it, we find scripture for daily reading, a listing of saint's days and other holy days throughout the year, and prayers for special occasions and for every meal.

Some Christians are uncomfortable with the very idea of a prayer book. In my long summer as a hospital chaplain, although I carried my prayer book with me everywhere I went, I was sometimes asked to "pray my own prayer" by people in despair who didn't see how words written by someone else could offer them strength and courage. But in the yearly retreat I co-lead for Baptist pastors and seminarians, I've seen how people who say they don't care for liturgical worship can also be fed by these beautiful words, by prayers that have been prayed for generations, by a creed that has been recited for centuries. At the end of our week together, we do a slimmed-down, slightly more ecumenical version of the Book of Common Prayer Eucharist, and these preachers and seminarians who in their own churches rarely experience "The Lord's Supper" are visibly moved by receiving the bread and wine (okay—grape juice; they are really Baptist) and by the language of the ministration: "The body of Christ, the bread of Heaven."

Those prayers written by others, my Baptist co-teacher the Reverend Dr. Hulitt Gloer reminds us during our week of study and worship, can become our prayers as well, and sometimes they will be the very words of our hearts. Moreover, as he tells our students, even for those who have been taught to pray extemporaneously, these are prayers we can offer when we don't know what to pray, or are too tired to pray, or are too broken to pray. The prayer book is there to guide us into deeper communion with God and with each other.

To anyone who might imagine that praying from the Book of Common Prayer is an act of laziness or a reflection of shallow faith, scholar and former bishop N. T. Wright would (and does) forcefully argue the precise opposite:

> There is nothing wrong, nothing sub-Christian . . . about using words, set forms, prayers and sequences of prayers written by other people in other centuries. Indeed, the idea that I must always find my own words, that I must generate my devotion from scratch every morning, that unless I think of new words I must be spiritually lazy or deficient—that has the all-too-familiar sign of human pride, of "doing it my way.". . . Good liturgy can be, should be, a sign of grace, an occasion of humility (accepting that someone else has said, better than I can, what I deeply want to express) and gratitude.[6]

All these gifts of the English tradition—a deeply incarnational spirituality that offers an everyday experience of the holy, a beautifully written prayer book that presents us with a powerful way to encounter God and each other, and the awareness that we are called to participate in something larger than our own petty concerns—are brought to us courtesy of something called the *via media*, the middle way, which Anglicans have sought to navigate first between Reformation Protestantism and Roman Catholicism, and later between other differing paths while seeking a workable center based on common worship. The things that engage me most about being Episcopalian seem to grow out of our ongoing attempt to balance useful elements from various traditions without going too far in any one direction. The *via media* is what makes Episcopalians simultaneously Protestant and Catholic, a people who value both word and sacrament, and it too suggests a worldview in which working out our salvation together is more important than being doctrinally pure.

The Right Reverend Rowan Williams, past archbishop of Canterbury and one of the world's great theologians, said in an e-mail from Cambridge that what the Anglican tradition tries to navigate on a daily basis is actually quite difficult, and certainly amazing when you think about it:

> The Anglican ideal is a family of local churches bound together by a shared structure and a shared style of worship and prayer grounded in the beliefs of the historic creeds in the light of which we read and hear Scripture. So we try to balance quite a lot of not-easily-balanced things. We want to be a Catholic body (i.e., a body with

real worldwide relationships and interdependence) but not cen-
tralised and coercive. We want to be Reformed (i.e. self-critical and
capable of change, but not simply a set of local communities ready
to spin apart and create new differences). We want to be traditional,
listening to the wisdom we inherit from the first centuries, living
within the great framework of belief in a threefold God, and in the
once-and-for-all embodiment of one dimension of that God in the
flesh and blood of Jesus—the basic creedal orthodoxy. We want to
be reading the Bible in that framework and in the company of those
who believe in the Trinity and the Incarnation. And we want the
Bible to be the final test for the integrity of what we say and do,
without making it an idol or a sort of written constitution. Hard
work! But if all these elements of Christian identity (liturgy, creeds,
Bible, relationship with God and all God's people) matter as they do,
then an adult Christianity will have to find ways of holding them
together. Anglicanism has tried the risky experiment of doing this
without too many structural rules, relying on the power of Christ-
centred relation.

To be Anglican, then, is to seek at the same time to be Catholic, yet
Reformed, to believe that sermons change hearts and minds but that the
Eucharist also preaches, to balance the diverse and potentially polarizing
elements of faith, and to navigate a way between extremes. Lord Williams
says that the difficulty comes because we rely too much on one aspect
or another: "The danger is of abstracting one bit of the map and making
it the whole picture—just being 'Biblical,' just being 'traditional,' just
being 'relevant' or 'contemporary.' " Too much of even a good thing, then,
can be detrimental to the health of the larger body, so balance in all things
is an Anglican ideal.

This idea of a balanced *via media* is developed powerfully at different times in our history. We can extrapolate it from the work of Richard
Hooker, one of the Anglican tradition's great theologians. We find it in
the so-called parliamentary "Elizabethan Settlement" (which described
the English Church as a Catholic body separate from Rome yet not fully
Calvinist, something strangely in between those two poles, and marked
by tolerance for those who disagreed, provided they didn't flout the law

or preach sedition), and in the writing and teaching of the Tractarians who made up the nineteenth-century Oxford Movement.

In current Episcopal life few of us are wrestling with defining ourselves in opposition to the pope or to Genevan Protestantism, but many of us are still trying to figure out where we stand on great issues of the day, on styles of worship, and on matters of faith and practice. The *via media* can help us all to live with others seeking their own answers. The Reverend Richard Pelkey, a priest in Florida, remarks that what we do well in the tradition, when we do it right, is to espouse "an ecclesiology that values relationships. It gives the space to allow for diversity and a spirit of generosity towards difference." The Reverend Jason Haddox, a priest from Augusta, Georgia, also notes how espousing a middle way allows diversity to flourish: "At our best, we stretch out to make room for as many different kinds of folks as possible. Even those we don't necessarily agree with about everything." Finally, Bill Tompson, a lay leader of the American Cathedral in Paris, France, agrees with this inclusive formula passionately:

> We are bound in fellowship by Baptism and the Eucharist—not by common assent to specific theological formulae or submission to some institution empowered to tell us what is and is not acceptable belief. The question we ask of those who come through our doors is not "Do you believe what we believe?" It is "Would you like to join with us sinners as we pray and break bread before our Lord together?"

Relationship is, then, the ultimate result of a balanced Anglican spirituality. It emerges from the emphasis on shared worship and prayer, and it is reinforced by our preference for a way between extremes. I received daily practical lessons about the importance of the middle way and of common worship as a way of bridging otherwise unbridgeable gaps when I was a seminarian at the Episcopal Theological Seminary of the Southwest in Austin, Texas. It became clear during our very first week together that my seminary class was an incredibly diverse group. We were gathered from all across America, from Massachusetts and Colorado, from Wyoming and Florida, from Alabama and Tennessee and Missouri and

Texas. Prior to seminary we had been professors (I still was, and unlike
the others, would continue to be), youth ministers, factory workers, pho-
tographers, anthropologists, and mechanics. We were all over the map
theologically, culturally, politically, and liturgically. Given my upbring-
ing in an intolerant religious tradition, I feared that we were in for three
years of disastrous dissension.

But I didn't account for the genius of the Anglican tradition, the
bringing together of many voices under one roof for the purpose of common prayer. During the course of our three years, we prayed together,
we took the Eucharist together, we broke bread in each other's houses,
we swam together, we camped together, we played music together (and
for each other), we ate together, we drank together, we laughed together,
and we wept together. My friends who differed radically from me became
valuable checks on my own excesses and on my own tendency to believe
I am absolutely right. I hope I served that function for them half as well
as they did for me.

During our three years together, I learned to listen to opposing views
with tolerance because I had accepted that all of us were brothers and
sisters, held together by our belief that we were called to be together by
something much larger than our own little desires, beliefs, and opinions.
As Bishop Jefferts Schori put it so beautifully above, "a holy and whole
and healed life seeks the flourishing and well-being of the rest, not ourselves alone." Seminary helped me to internalize this important Anglican
lesson about placing the well-being of others over myself.

The Anglican approaches to moderation and community would also
seem to have a lot to offer a society that currently seems to be filled with
people shouting their dissenting views at each other from opposite sides
of the canyon. When we recognize, as the *via media* does, that somewhere
in between two poles the majority of us can live and work together, it
reminds us that we need not die in every ditch for our beliefs. Others—
friends, sisters and brothers in Christ—do not hold our views, and they
do so for reasons that seem logical to them. And yet we are called to love
them—as they are called, thanks be to God, to love us.

Religion can be a divisive force and spirituality can be an individual
affection, but when shaped by the Anglican tradition, we find both of

them urging us into community, building tolerance and helping us to practice love. These are all ways in which the Anglican way can thus shine a light on our everyday journey.

We have been given a tradition in which we need not take our ball and go home, for we know from experience that the game is richer when we all bring our different talents and passions to it. This tradition of common worship can be painfully hard to do—I've read about more than one Church of England synod (a national convention) marked by dissension, sat in more than one local church committee meeting marked by outright hostility—but common worship is our own particular calling (what the Apostle Paul speaks of as "charisms" or gifts of the spirit) we can offer the world. Lory Hunt, the youth minister from the other Paris (the one in Texas) brings all of this chapter's elements together when she says that the gift of the Anglican tradition comes down to "the liturgy of worship. The structure and language speaks to me and transcends my little piece of the world to the larger communion of saints." When we come to the table of Christ together, we bear witness to a broken world that wholeness and reconciliation are not only possible, but to be hoped for. When we are able to love across boundaries, it offers an example to the world that differences need not separate us.

In that search for balance and reconciliation that are at the heart of Anglican faith and practice, Episcopalians are continuing to evidence the great practices of the traditions from which we sprang. From the Catholic tradition we take our continued love for beauty and liturgy, our commitment to daily prayer, our belief that we encounter God in formal sacraments, our structure of deacons, priests, and bishops. From the Protestant Reformation we take our call to read and digest scripture, our desire to think for ourselves, our love of worship in our own language, our democratic polity. But in all things, reconciliation, a "both/and" approach rather than an "either/or" spirit infuses us. In the face of a culture that often calls itself spiritual but not religious, Episcopalians offer the possibility that one can be both—and that by living out our faith daily, we can make a spiritual and substantial difference in the world around us.

Questions for Discussion

1. What does it mean, as David Sugeno asks, to pursue a Christianity shaped by an English identity? Do you see differences between English and American culture?
2. What does the Book of Common Prayer offer to those in the Anglican and Episcopal traditions? Does our orientation around common worship differ from what holds other denominations together?
3. What does inclusiveness mean to you? Tolerance? When, in your experience, have you seen an institution bring together diverse people under one roof?
4. How have you found it possible to avoid being an extremist on issues that don't truly matter in the long run? How have you found it possible (or impossible) to be in close proximity to those who don't think as you do?

For Further Reading

Frank Griswold, *Praying Our Days: A Guide and Companion* (New York: Morehouse, 2009).

Bishop Griswold, Bishop Jefferts Schori's predecessor as presiding bishop, is also a talented and deeply committed teacher of Christian spirituality. In this small book, he pulls together resources for daily and hourly prayer from Anglican prayer books and from across the Christian tradition, and offers a unique resource for Episcopal devotion.

Geoffrey Rowell, Kenneth Stevenson, and Rowan Williams, *Love's Redeeming Work: The Anglican Quest for Holiness* (Oxford, UK: Oxford University Press, 2004).

The editors have gathered in this anthology selections on holiness by Anglican luminaries from Thomas Cranmer and William Tyndale to modern figures like C. S. Lewis and the Welsh poet R. S. Thomas. It's a treasure trove of Anglican spirituality.

Rowan Williams, *Anglican Identities* (Cambridge, MA: Cowley, 2004).

In this collection of essays, the former archbishop of Canterbury explores the thought and theology of seminal figures in the Anglican tradition, among them William Tyndale, Richard Hooker, George Herbert, and William Temple, all in service of a larger question: What does it mean to be Anglican?

Living the Questions: A Faith That Stays Open All Night

Afew weeks ago my wife, Jeanie, and I were sitting in the choir stall at the American Cathedral in Paris for the 9 a.m. service. The dean of the cathedral, the Very Reverend Lucinda Laird, stepped into our midst to preach, and she began her sermon by asking some hard questions. She had just lived through a very trying week: One of her dearest friends had died without warning, and on top of that, a lovely and loving couple she had married early in her life as a priest had just announced that they were getting a divorce. I imagine that it must have felt like a wave of unexpected heartbreak washing over her and threatening to knock her off her feet. Certainly it was apparent that the deaths of her friend and of her friends' marriage had strongly affected her.

What are we supposed to do, Dean Laird asked us, with such bad news, with the tragedies life throws at us all too often? What do scripture, faith, and our tradition have to say to us—if anything—about life's hard questions?

As we listened, Dean Laird began to wrestle with those questions in front of our very eyes, began to peel back the layers of faith and suffering to get at some answers. She did this by thinking through the scriptures assigned in the day's lectionary readings. She did it by consulting her own considerable intelligence as she walked us through some provisional answers about how and what suffering is for those who love God.

By the time she was finished, we all had reached some answers—provisional ones, perhaps, but certainly situated on solid footing—and gained some peace that God was present in all that transpires, and that God's love will never fail us.

I also know a bit about the public wrestling with hard questions that is a vital part of the faith and practice of the Episcopal Church. I am often asked to teach and to preach, whether in my home church or in other settings around the world. When I am preparing to wrestle, I have a procedure I've learned to follow: I sit down in my office at the Episcopal Seminary of the Southwest where all my theological books are shelved. I read through the biblical texts associated with my sermon or with my topic, more than once, usually some weeks ahead of time. I read these passages in several translations and examine the important Greek or Hebrew words so I can be sure I'm getting at the original nuances of the scriptures.

I read commentaries on these passages, often the writings of other thinkers in the history of the Church: Augustine, John Wesley, John Calvin. I want to know what people in the past have thought about what I'm studying, because I am entering into a conversation that has been going on for centuries, and I am not the first person wrestling with them. I also read contemporary commentaries and scholarly treatments that illuminate history, theology, pastoral concerns.

And finally, I sit, and I think. I sit, I think, and I go on thinking. I think about the hard questions while I'm driving to my teaching job at Baylor, one hundred miles each way. I think about it when I'm on my bike, or on the elliptical machine working out. I think about it when I'm outside, next to the water. (Greg Rickel taught me the joy of writing your sermons at Austin's Barton Springs.)

What I'm doing as I read, think, talk with others, and write, is what Lucinda Laird was doing in her sermon at the American Cathedral: Episcopal theology. Another of the great legacies of the Anglican tradition we discussed in Chapter One is a way of doing theology (literally, "theology" just means "talk about God") that is distinctive to Anglicans and Episcopalians.

Richard Hooker was an early proponent of a sort of three-pronged approach to revelation—he is often (mistakenly) said to have described the process of weighing scripture, reason, and the Church's teaching as a "three-legged" stool, in which each of the three legs is necessary and none can be "longer" than the other lest the stool topple over! The three-legged stool is clearly another example of the Anglican *via media*. Unlike Catholics, we don't give the Church and its authorities the last word, and unlike Protestants, we don't imagine that our individual readings of scripture, however guided by the Holy Spirit, represent the sole truth. The beauty of the concept, of course, is that these three things in concert allow us to enter into the long, ongoing conversation of theology without overemphasizing one mode of understanding over another. It is Anglican balance at work.

Some contemporary Christian traditions privilege scripture over any other means of knowing God. For them, the scriptures are God-breathed, and every word, verse, and chapter are to be interpreted as simply and literally as possible, even if these interpretations tend to come at the expense of the larger story of the Bible. It is possible to read the Bible as monolithic, infallible, and inerrant—although you then are forced to try to justify every contradiction and accept every verse as equally authoritative. This becomes a house of cards that collapses in a heap if you pull out any one of them, and represents a way of reading the Bible that doesn't consider it as a cultural document, nor as a collection of texts in conversation with each other. Why do the gospels differ in some essentials? Why (to choose one variance) is Jesus's ministry variously said to be one year long and three years long?

Could it be that the writers of the gospels were less interested in advancing a unified story (why write four identical gospels?) than they were in exploring different understandings of Jesus that seemed most pertinent to the communities for which they wrote?

Episcopal scholars like Marcus Borg (Canon Theologian at Portland's Trinity Episcopal Cathedral) have long advocated taking the Bible seriously—but reading it better. To read it as a recipe book or an owner's manual in which every section is as important as every other section doesn't seem possible to many of us in the twenty-first century. How can Bible verses justifying slavery, condemning homosexuality, or limiting the roles of women in the Church be authoritative in a world that has largely moved beyond those notions? (For that matter, how can we keep from collapsing in helpless laughter, as current Archbishop of Canterbury Justin

Welby did when asked to read from the lectern the Old Testament pro-
scriptions against eating shellfish, vultures, camels, and rock badgers?)

N. T. Wright wrote *Simply Christian* to justify the sort of thoughtful
and engaged Christianity we seek in the Episcopal Church. He certainly
thinks the Bible is important; after all, Wright is perhaps the world's leading scholar of the New (or Christian) Testament. But in his book, he comes
to the Bible only in Chapter Thirteen—after chapters on justice, beauty,
God, the people of God, and Jesus. Wright advocates a serious study of the
Bible (unlike some progressive Christians, he actually believes that the miracles narrated in it took place), but reason and the traditions of the Church
have to be used as filters to reading it. "Squabbling over particular defini-
tions of the qualities of the Bible is like a married couple squabbling over
who love the children more, when they should be getting on with bringing them up and setting them a good example. The Bible is there to enable
God's people to be equipped to do God's work in God's world, not to give
them an excuse to sit back smugly, knowing they possess all God's truth."[7]

The Very Reverend Martyn Percy, Dean of Christ Church, Oxford,
has, he likes to say, gotten free lunch for years for his brief appearance in
Dan Brown's *The DaVinci Code*. That blockbuster novel quotes Dean Percy
saying—as he sometimes does in interviews or in the media—that "The
Bible did not arrive by fax from heaven."

What he means, he says, is that history reveals that God can only be
known provisionally. To imagine that we, so to speak, possess all God's
truth, that God's truth is transferred through the Bible like some sort of
spiritual IV, is to miss how God is being revealed to us in the scriptures. In
his book *Thirty-Nine New Articles*, Dean Percy writes that "the Bible does
indeed contain many things that God may want to say to humanity. . . .
But it also contains opinions about God (even one or two moans and com-
plaints—see the Psalms); it contains allegory, parables, humour, histories
and debates. The nature of the Bible invites us to contemplate the very
many ways in which God speaks to us."[8]

We are never given full knowledge of who God is. Indeed, classi-
cal theology would tell us that we are incapable of grasping who God
is even if God were to directly reveal God's self to us. Moreover, any
belief that one can understand the Bible without the effort of interpret-
ing it flies in the face of how the Church has traditionally understood

biblical interpretation. Some things in scripture, as Augustine of Hippo noted over 1500 years ago, we are meant to understand literally; some we are meant to understand metaphorically. And, as good Episcopalians, Christian tradition and reason help us discern which is which.

But although most Episcopal and Anglican scholars and theologians agree that the Bible is not transparent, no one should imagine that the Bible is somehow unimportant to us. It is at the center of our faith. Remember what Rowan Williams said: "We want the Bible to be the final test for the integrity of what we say and do, without making it an idol or a sort of written constitution." Every Sunday, Episcopal and Anglican services are packed full of scripture: usually a reading from the Old Testament, a Psalm, a New Testament reading, and a gospel reading. In the course of a year, someone attending church will hear a vast selection of the Bible, not just the pastor's favorite passages.

The Revised Common Lectionary, which Episcopalians employ in worship (along with the Roman Catholic Church, the Lutheran Church, and other liturgical traditions), follows a three-year cycle that takes us all the way through one of the Synoptic Gospels (that is, Matthew, Mark, or Luke) each year. Meanwhile, the Gospel of John is read in huge chunks during the holiest times on our calendar—in Advent, Lent, and Holy Week.

And these passages read during an Episcopal service aren't asked to survive in a vacuum. They interact with the liturgy (often the prayer book collect or the prayers of the people will echo themes from the readings), and the preacher explores them for the community in her or his sermon. While Episcopalians may not know the Bible "chapter and verse" as some Bible-believing Christians do, they have a strong sense of the Bible's overarching themes of God's reaching out to humanity, and of our faithful—and ever changing—responses to that offer of relationship. As Donna Johnson, a writer and Episcopal layperson in Austin, says, one of our gifts is "the ability to allow the Christian story to evolve—while maintaining its traditions." Episcopalians value being invited to wrestle for meaning, to engage in conversations that don't assume a finished answer. Loren Peters, an Episcopal hospice chaplain in Everett, Washington, says he loves that we have "a regard for Truth that promotes thoughtfulness rather than certainty."

The three-legged stool offers us a model for asking hard questions and searching for the answers together. This model treats the problem of discerning who God is and what God wants of us as a process, not as a list of settled propositions. The Anglican tradition actually offers considerable freedom in the results people get when they do theology. People who believe the virgin birth is literally true and people who believe that the virgin birth is a nice metaphor for the unique stature of Jesus can (and do) pray next to each other every week. What we accept as essential dogma is incorporated in the Apostle's Creed or the Nicene Creed, one of which is regularly recited in our worship. Everything else is up for conversation.

The creeds serve as our theological gathering point. Like the Baptismal Covenant, which we reaffirm several times a year when we welcome new people into the body of Christ, we repeat the creeds as a way of reaffirming the common salvation narrative we claim. What we mean by those phrases is something we must wrestle with, but we do so in a community that says these words together and seeks their meaning together.

Briefly, the creeds remind us that we believe in a single God experienced in three persons—Father, Son, and Holy Spirit. We believe that a first-century Jewish peasant named Jesus was the son of God and simultaneously of the same substance as God (the historic creeds mostly exist to wrestle with the brain-busting idea of Jesus' human and divine natures). We believe in the Spirit of God that binds us together; we believe in the one Church of God and its believers scattered across the globe; we look for a future beyond death when we will be with God, "the life of the world to come" where Jesus will rule over a kingdom that has no end.

Beyond that outline of faith, everything is up for discussion, and discuss it we do. Some of us even wrestle with the creeds. The Right Reverend John Shelby Spong, popular writer and retired bishop of Newark, walks through the Nicene Creed phrase by phrase in *Why Christianity Must Change or Die* and explains why he thinks almost every article of faith we recite in the Nicene Creed is ridiculous. Discussion and debate are a part of Episcopal life. Since the heart of our tradition is common worship instead of common belief, we gather to help each other sort out what we believe. We discuss God in formal classes and small groups, over coffee and at Theology on Tap (I have participated in my share of events bringing together hops and holiness), in Education for Ministry (EfM) classes, and at the church door, where we brace the preacher with a question about her sermon.

Theological education and discussion are a part of our common life together, a form of continuing preparation to which all of the baptized are called. Andy Doyle told me over coffee one morning that one of his priorities as bishop was to get every Episcopalian in the Diocese of Texas doing theology. Presiding Bishop Katharine Jefferts Schori expands on that. She says that every Episcopalian everywhere should be involved in the work of theology: "The Episcopal Church believes that all its members need to be well-formed and well-educated for the baptismal ministry we share in the Body of Christ. Theological education for all is an essential foundation for baptismal ministry. . . . All congregations are further encouraged to develop and promote opportunities for the education of all members from small children to our most senior elders. As we haven't yet reached the fullness of the Reign of God, we all have something to learn!"[9]

Theology in the Anglican/Episcopal tradition, then, isn't something that is limited to academics and church leaders. Although I might spend hours preparing to preach, after delivering my sermon, I stand at the door, and talk to parishioners about what I've just said. Sometimes I'm greeted with thanks and agreement; sometimes I'm greeted with a challenging question or a furrowed brow, and I am never offended by that. Unlike those Christian traditions where a pope or a pastor gives the final word for a body of believers, all Episcopalians are invited—indeed, expected—to think for themselves.

Here are a few pointers on how Episcopalians might approach that task: We can read scripture for ourselves and talk about it with others, of course, but when we do theology, we should recognize that we are entering into that larger conversation that has been going on for centuries. All of us know that it is bad manners to assume that nothing that was said before we walked into the room was important, so it's often a good idea to find out what others talked about before we arrived.

When I'm trying to catch up on the conversation, I poke my head into several different rooms, starting with my own. The Anglican/Episcopal way has had some notable theological voices—we have mentioned Richard Hooker, and other great past theologians and apologists worth reading, ordained and lay, include William Law, Lancelot Andrewes, C. S. Lewis, and Dorothy Sayers. Today, our tradition boasts preachers, teachers, scholars, and writers like Barbara Brown Taylor, Marcus Borg, Kathleen Tanner, N. T. Wright, Mary C. Earle, Desmond Tutu, Frederick Schmidt, Robin Griffith-Jones, Martyn Percy, Sara Miles, and perhaps the world's most distinguished living theologian, Rowan Williams.

I always want to know what my fellow travelers have been talking about before I enter the conversation. But I don't stop there. The Anglican tradition has never shut out other voices just because we can't claim them as our own. We pay attention to the Desert Fathers and Mothers, to the great Doctors of the Church such as Augustine and Aquinas, to Catholic, Protestant, and Orthodox voices as well as our Anglicans. We listen to contemporary voices who might offer as much wisdom as the voices of the distant past. All of that is important. When we try to discern how God is speaking, we should not assume that God is speaking only through the narrow channels of our own thinkers, even if their powerful works often hold special meaning for us. I find myself frequently opening Rowan Williams's *Tokens of Trust* or *Resurrection* to make sense of what I believe about God and why. But while Rowan Williams is my favorite theologian, I also hear God speaking in the ancient words of the African Catholic theologian Tertullian and in the modern words of the Lutheran pastor Nadia Bolz-Weber. If we're serious about the idea of the *via media*, then even here the Anglican tradition should be seeking to mediate, to synthesize, to find the best way forward from a variety of possibilities.

Let me walk you through how we might do Anglican theology. Let's take a timeless yet contemporary problem like poverty, which is both a political and a theological issue over which Christians disagree. Some American Christians believe that since multiple gospels quote Jesus as saying that "the poor will always be with you," we shouldn't try to solve poverty. From this, they conclude that it would be wrong to devote too much attention to solving this problem if Jesus is prophesying that we will never rid the world of it. Do some good work among the poor, maybe ask your church to feed the starving. Diminish the suffering where you find it. That seems "Jesusy." But the Bible says it, I believe it, that settles it. Some people will always be poor. Who am I to argue with Jesus?

Doing Episcopal theology on this issue would see us considering more than that single verse, though. We would probably note that more than two thousand verses of the Bible speak directly to the issue of poverty, while the overarching story of God we find in the Bible suggests that God is to be found with the starving, the broken, the alien, and the homeless. As Archbishop Desmond Tutu might say, our God has a preference for the poor. In addition to consulting Tutu, we might incorporate reading an encyclical from the pope on poverty. We might rely on a work from Augustine that spells out the Church's notions of compassion and charity or a sermon from former Episcopal Presiding Bishop John Hines that reminds us that the Church is an agent of God's reconciling love, and, as such, cannot stand by when people suffer.

Alongside those luminaries, we might also listen to the voices of our fellow travelers who have reached the theological conclusion that we must be where the oppressed are, that we are always called to offer God's hope to the hopeless, and that we are called to overhaul a system that dictates that some should starve while others feast. So we might consider the witness of the saints of our tradition like William Wilberforce, who helped overthrow the supreme injustice of the British slave trade, or Episcopal seminarian Jonathan Myrick Daniels, who died fighting for civil rights in the Deep South. As we're reading scripture, as we're participating in the larger conversation, we might also consult our own reason, which tells us that it is unjust for some to starve while others feast—and, lo and behold, we have just done theology. We reached a conclusion together (Episcopalians believe we discern in community) thoughtfully, responsibly, the Episcopal way. In this exercise, our theological conclusion might be that ending poverty should be the goal of everyone who calls him- or herself a Christian, a conclusion reached by our reading of scripture, by our understanding of the tradition, and by our own good brains.

Now, some have suggested we might add a fourth leg to the stool, that of personal revelation. In some Christian traditions, individual revelation is of real importance, and, as we'll see in a few chapters, the Episcopal Church values beauty and cultural expressions, so we do believe that God may still be speaking through the world outside the scriptures. If we take individual revelation as a part of our process of theological reasoning, though, we have to be careful to treat it with the same seriousness we do the other legs, to regard it as a part of a process that cannot unbalance the others, and to offer our individual revelation for community discernment.

Some people who claim to have gained individual revelations allow the emotion or immediacy of that message to overbalance every other factor. It's difficult, as many of my clergy friends know, to respond to the statement that "God told me to do this."

Any individual revelation we may believe we have been given through prayer, worship, or by our close attention to the world around us also has to fit in with biblical revelation, with the voices of our tradition, and with the dictates of reason. I recall my single instance of receiving a vision (at least, I thought it was a vision; it could also have been sleep deprivation or an unhappy combination of anti-depression meds). In that revelation, God told me that I was going to get something I very much wanted. Now, that vision didn't much fit the facts on the ground, and it didn't ultimately turn out to be true. But it does suggest something important about individual revelation. Oftentimes people who hear God speaking hear things they want to hear. I, for one, would be more convinced if they heard messages such as God offered to Abraham and Jonah, a voice speaking commands that were counter to their own desires, but clearly in line with God's purpose.

On the other hand, as suspicious as I might seem about our hearing the voice of God, I do believe that God can speak—and is speaking—to us outside of scripture, reason, and tradition. I have written often about the movie *Pulp Fiction*, for example, a vile and violent meditation on the power of grace. *Pulp Fiction* sustained me in belief in God at a time when I was entirely outside the Christian tradition. As unchristian as some of its subject matter might be, *Pulp Fiction* helped me wrestle with some hard questions at a time when I really needed theology to stay alive. As I understood the tradition and the scriptures then, as I applied my reason, I believed that God offers grace to unworthy sinners. *Pulp Fiction* seconded those conclusions and made them dramatic so that I could live them. Every major character in *Pulp Fiction* is extended the possibility of grace; two of them actually escape town on a motorcycle called Grace.

What the movie said to me was that it isn't about whether we are good or bad, because even when I wasn't a Christian I believed in sin in all of its manifestations. We are all going to do things we shouldn't. But the larger question is whether or not we are willing to accept the grace we are offered and live into the new life it requires.

If we go on the way we've been living, then, like John Travolta's Vincent Vega, we will die. But if we accept the possibility that God might be moving in our lives—even moving miraculously, as Samuel Jackson's Jules believes—then we can change. We can try—real hard—to stop being the tyranny of evil men, and try real hard to be the shepherd.

If, as we believe, God is still moving in the world, then revelation didn't stop 1900 years ago when the last canonical books of the Bible were written, and it didn't stop in 1994, when *Pulp Fiction* was released. God is still speaking, as we will explore in more detail, through our worship, through the truth and beauty to be found in the world outside the walls of the church, and in our attempts to live out our beliefs in community.

We wrestle with the hard questions in all those ways. They, too, are Episcopal theology.

Questions for Discussion

1. What do you imagine when you hear the words "theology" and "theologian"? Have you ever thought of yourself as a theologian?
2. What do you believe the Bible to be? Is it authoritative for you? What gives it that authority?
3. Do you have a favorite theologian or spiritual writer? What about her or him captures your imagination?
4. Have you ever received something you would call a revelation from God? What were the circumstances? How did you decide whether or not it was worth believing?

For Further Reading

Marcus Borg, *Reading the Bible Again for the First Time* (New York: HarperOne, 2002).

Professor Borg offers the persuasive thesis in this book that instead of reading the Bible in tiny bits and pieces and arguing about what they mean, we should pay attention to the overarching narrative of the Bible: God's love for humanity and our reactions to that love.

Greg Garrett, *The Other Jesus: Rejecting a Religion of Fear for the God of Love* (Louisville, KY: Westminster John Knox Press, 2011).

In this book on an engaged twenty-first century Christianity, I expand on the idea that we are called to do theology as a part of our own faith and practice, and suggest ways we might understand the Bible, the tradition, and individual revelation as a part of that practice.

Cynthia Briggs Kittredge, *Conversations with Scripture: The Gospel of John* (New York: Morehouse, 2007).

Seminary dean and renowned New Testament scholar Cynthia Kittredge leads readers through an informed and accessible study of the Gospel of John, bringing her scholarly tools to bear on a text she argues is marked by deep generosity.

Rowan Williams, *Tokens of Trust: An Introduction to Christian Belief* (Louisville, KY: Westminster John Knox, 2010).

In perhaps his most useful and accessible work of theology, the former archbishop of Canterbury explores the historic creeds to argue that God is worthy of our trust and belief, that Jesus' life and death reveal him as perfect love made human, and that we meet God most fully in the company of others.

Worship and Community: One Way God Touches and Heals Us

One of the most popular stories of our time is being unfolded in George R. R. Martin's *Song of Ice and Fire* books, which to date have sold over twenty-five million copies, been translated into forty languages, and been adapted into *A Game of Thrones*, one of the most honored shows in television history. Faith and belief are major elements of this saga—belief in the Old Gods, or the New Gods, or the Lord of Light—and Martin himself has talked about parallels between faith in and worship of the seven New Gods (actually seven facets of a single deity) and the faith and worship of the medieval Roman Catholic Church.

In the second novel in the series, *A Clash of Kings*, we find a scene where on the eve of a major battle, Sansa, a teenage girl from the noble Stark family, is drawn by the sound of singing into a church or "sept" in the kingdom's major city, King's Landing. The scene is described as being very much like walking into a cathedral or a beautiful historic church today: Candles are lit, light streams through stained glass, and the space is filled by a gathering of people who would not normally gather.

King's Landing is normally a place where rigid divisions are enforced between noble and common, knights and mercenaries, rich and poor. But on this occasion, after Sansa lights a candle to honor each of the aspects of the One God, she finds herself squeezing in between an aged washwoman and a young boy dressed in fine linen, and joins them in singing a hymn asking the Mother to spare the sons who are fighting (and the

daughters who will inevitably suffer rape and degradation in a defeat).
Sansa lifts her voice in song, we are told, "with grizzled old serving men
and anxious young wives, with serving girls and soldiers, cooks and fal-
coners, knights and knaves, squires and spit boys and nursing mothers.
She sang with those inside the castle walls and those without, sang with
all the city. She sang for mercy, for the living and the dead alike."[10]

In a dark world filled with strife and division, greed and hatred, people from all walks of life come together for a prayer service in the sept,
and there they find comfort and community. It's a remarkable reminder
from popular culture of the power of worship to bring people together
and to offer at least momentary insights that we are much more alike than
we are different.

Worship changes people.

All the same, I used to despise Psalm 122 when I was a kid. That's the
psalm that began, "I was glad when they said unto me, Let us go into the
house of the LORD" (KJV). It was one of those popular Bible verses that
nonetheless didn't ring true to my experience—and doesn't ring true to
many people, I fear.

Partly I wasn't glad to go into the house of the Lord because I was a
kid, and we went to church a lot. I would rather have been outside playing—and some nights, I snuck out of prayer meetings and climbed onto
the roof of the church, wandered its dark hallways, and had adventures.

But partly it was because even at that young age I didn't like the
house of the Lord in which I was raised. I liked singing some of the songs,
which were classic gospel or bluegrass hymns. I found comfort in some
of the repeated phrases and practices (like the benediction sung at the
end of every service in our church in Charlotte, "The Lord bless you and
keep you"). But for the most part, I wasn't drawn to our worship (which
emphasized emotion and immediate experience), the long sermons (which
consisted of an opening joke and then verse by verse explication of a
Bible passage), or the interminable altar calls (in which a sanctuary full of
people, all of whom claimed to love Jesus, were forced to suffer through
one verse after another, one challenge after another, until our pastor was
absolutely certain that everyone in the building had every opportunity
to come to the front of the church and publicly repent of her or his sins).

Like many other people I know, I left the tradition I grew up in because I didn't feel connected to it. I didn't feel that it connected me to God. And, although I don't think I could have articulated this then, I didn't feel connected to the people with whom I worshipped.

I was one of the massive throng who left organized religion. But I was fortunate in that eventually I stumbled onto another tradition that did make me feel connected to God and other human beings, and I found it at a time when I desperately needed that sense of connection.

It's not overly dramatic to say that becoming a worshipper at St. James' Episcopal Church saved my life.

In the years 2001 and 2002, I was a mess, a barely together trash bag crammed full of grief and despair. I didn't know what I was going to do, and I didn't know how much longer I could go on doing it. I certainly didn't expect that I would find relief and meaning in the house of the Lord. But at a time when I felt completely alone and at loose ends, at a time when I really couldn't see a reason to go on living, I walked into this unfamiliar church, and its unfamiliar worship service gave me something I had never felt before. Peace.

Maybe you too know what it feels like to be lost, alone, searching for something. My story sounds similar to many others I've heard over the years. Americans seem to be unhappy, at loose ends, lonely as we've never been before. We overeat, overdrink, over-consume, and overmedicate ourselves. Although we have hundreds of channels of cable television, millions of pages of information on the Internet, TV shows on demand, instant chat, e-mail and video messaging, we still sometimes feel as though we're alone in the world.

How's that for irony? Despite the fact that we are at least potentially better connected to each other than at any other time in history—I can call a friend in Africa from Wales, check his Facebook status, tweet a picture to him—many of us feel more disconnected than ever before. We need something. But what?

A few years back, Robert B. Putnam's best seller *Bowling Alone* offered a provocative thesis: Our greatest problem as a culture, it said, is that we no longer do things in community. Fewer and fewer Americans eat dinner together, belong to clubs or go to meetings, even have friends over.

The title came from one of Putnam's most interesting factoids: that even though more of us are bowling, we are even bowling alone.

When people no longer feel a connection to others, the fabric of our society unravels, and *Bowling Alone* is far from the only voice to suggest that our loss of community is damaging us emotionally and spiritually. In 2011, Lillian Daniels wrote a much-read *Huffington Post* column called "Spiritual but Not Religious? Please Stop Boring Me," and one of its laments was that the "spiritual but not religious" impulse simply represents American individualism at its worst. It isolates us. It creates people fundamentally lacking in the gifts proffered by community, among them courage. Her conclusion was that it even makes us boring:

> Being privately spiritual but not religious just doesn't interest me. There is nothing challenging about having deep thoughts all by oneself. What is interesting is doing this work in community, where other people might call you on stuff, or heaven forbid, disagree with you. Where life with God gets rich and provocative is when you dig deeply into a tradition that you did not invent all for yourself.[11]

So, sociologists measure it, pastors lament it, and atheists too recognize that our tendency toward solipsism damages us as human beings. In his best-selling book *Religion for Atheists*, Alain de Botton laments the many things that people of faith traditionally possess that all people ought to have. One of those things is community, most particularly a community made up of a variety of people drawn together from outside a person's normal limited circle of acquaintances—something like the community that Sansa Stark discovers in the sept in *A Clash of Kings*. And although de Botton finds church services illogical and frankly boring, he says that, of all things, the Eucharist offers the very best example of how to create community among a diverse body of people. By the end of the liturgy, he suggests—after the singing, the lessons, the sermon, the prayers, the bread and wine—participants should be shifted "at least fractionally off our accustomed egocentric axes." Its rigidly defined framework and its focus on a communal meal should, he argues, "inspire visitors to suspend their customary frightened egoism in favour of a joyful immersion in a collective spirit—an unlikely scenario in the majority of modern community centres, whose appearance paradoxically serves to confirm the inadvisability of joining anything communal."[12]

What common worship does—as even an atheist recognizes—is make something whole out of scattered individuals. It encourages them to drop their usual force fields holding everyone else at a distance.

That's what happens when Episcopalians come together to worship. We set aside a space where people come anticipating a certain thing to happen. By creating a setting, by making it a place where at a certain time, certain events occur, we tap into habit, ritual, functional fixedness (the linking of certain places with expected results). By bringing together a group of people gathered not because of their age, race, occupation, or wealth but because of their commitment to shared values and experience, the liturgy breaks down the divisions between us. By asking us to leave our worldly concerns at the door, the liturgy invites us all to consider something higher, nobler, more sacrificial than the values of the culture around us. And by providing us with comfort, courage, and community, it encourages us to believe we can actually attain that higher calling—together.

Lory Hunt argues that the fact of our worship together makes us part of something much larger than ourselves. For her, it matters "knowing that saints before (and all over the world) have prayed the same prayers. The cloud of witnesses is very real for me. Also, I like that the liturgy really is 'Liturgy,' the work of the people. It is participatory, not a spectator sport." As Lory points out, the Greek roots of "liturgy" do mean "work of the people," and, as with many Episcopalians, liturgy offers her a chance to participate actively in worship rather than feel preached at or entertained, to seek God rather than have God lobbed at her.

Rowan Williams still remembers his first instance of Anglican worship, "at the age of about eleven, in a local parish church: the first time I'd really sensed in church the power of a beauty not of our making. Not because of a great deal of fuss and ceremony, but in the quiet order and flow of an act that obviously grew out of profound attention to God's mystery." With its quiet order and flow, the Anglican tradition is uniquely suited to the bringing together of diverse people and creating community among them. When Archbishop Cranmer created the Book of Common Prayer, he was setting up a way of belief and practice centered not on creed or dogma (what do you believe?) or infallible leadership (who tells you what to believe?) but on common worship. In the Episcopal Church, we pray together, we take communion together, we stand up together, we kneel together, and, eventually, if we do all these things, we *are* together.

N. T. Wright says that we come together as the church for three reasons: to worship God, to work for God's kingdom in the world, and the third reason, which is interrelated with the first two, "to encourage one another, to build one another up in faith, to pray with and for one another, to learn from one another and teach one another, to set one another examples to follow, challenges to take up, and urgent tasks to perform."[13] Worship builds communities; worship offers a chance for worshippers to grow with and through their interaction with each other.

In the fall of 2008, I lived at the National Cathedral in Washington, DC, I was working on the book that became *The Other Jesus* while resident as a fellow at the cathedral's College of Preachers. At the end of every day of writing, I went up the hill to the cathedral, sat down in the choir (the section of the cathedral closest to the altar) and entered into the service of Evensong.

I spoke the words, I chanted the creed, I knelt for prayer, just like all the others gathered there. Most of the worshippers were tourists from around the world who wanted to experience the cathedral up close. But every evening I encountered some of the same people there in the choir, and we obviously were not gathering for Evensong because of our shared age, race, occupation, or wealth. I would guess that those of us who were regulars had very little in common besides the desire for comfort and connection.

Two congregants I saw daily were an elderly white gentleman, always dressed in the same gray three-piece suit, and a homeless African American woman carrying all her possessions in a plastic bag. After a week of worship together, they were nodding to me, and smiling at me. Then we began greeting each other before or after worship and I began to anticipate gathering with them. When I went back to Texas at the end of my fellowship, my worship-mates were among the things I missed most.

Likewise, when I am writing in Wales, I attend a morning Eucharist at Gladstone's Library. There, I am often the lone American voice raised among an array of other accents—Oxbridge, Irish, Scots, Northern English,

Londoner, and Australian. The other worshippers might be clergy, or students, or tourists. They might be faithful or merely curious. But for the length of that service, we are brothers and sisters. We stand and sit together, we pray together, we take communion together, and by the time the service is concluded, we feel our oneness. The service itself tells us this is true. We are one, the liturgy informs us, because we eat of the same bread, drink the same wine. And afterwards, we gather together for breakfast, share stories, and encourage each other in the work we are doing.

The liturgy may give us our truest example of *e pluribus unum*, "out of many, one." Our participation together moves us from a place of brokenness to a place of wholeness. Bishop Jeff Fisher of Texas writes that the breaking of the bread is his favorite moment in the liturgy because of what it symbolizes. "I have celebrated the Eucharist hundreds of times, yet when I break the bread, it always moves me: broken bread, broken Jesus, for broken people." In the liturgy, taking this broken bread with others like us is true worship.

Now, all churches worship, and I've talked with many other Christians about what they love about their churches. (And, of course, sometimes, what they hate, although people don't seem to stay long in churches that aren't a fit for them.) Some are moved in worship by the participatory element of music, whether singing great hymns or losing themselves in the repetition of praise choruses or hearing amazing instrumental music. Others find themselves caught up in preaching so inspirational or emotional you could hear a pin drop in the auditorium. Some value their small groups, an intimate gathering of people who know them by name, especially in larger faith communities. Some are attracted, frankly, by entertainment value: professional-quality music, lighting, and sound, an engaging preacher, a service that moves like lightning with never a dull moment.

You can find many of these elements in Episcopal Churches (although not, one supposes, a service that moves lickety-split without a moment for reflection). But as we've mentioned, it is the liturgy itself—the pattern of the service, from invitation to worship through the exploration of the scripture lessons and reflection of the sermon, through confession and greeting to the blessing and consumption of the bread and wine, and, finally, a blessing and a benediction releasing worshippers back into the world—that holds first place in the hearts of Episcopalians. The Reverend

Everett Lees, whose parish is in Tulsa, Oklahoma, puts "Holy Communion" first on the list of things he celebrates about the Episcopal Church. The Reverend Jim Trimble, who serves in Pewee Valley, just outside Louisville, Kentucky, cites "the liturgy, involving our work, prayers, and all our senses." And Diane Owens from Austin loves "bells and smells and the reverence for liturgy. When faith wavers, liturgy keeps you afloat."

Although all our services are built around a common pattern of liturgy, Episcopalians are not limited to one style of worship. My church demonstrates the smorgasbord of Episcopal services: On a typical Sunday at St. David's, we offer a short spoken Eucharist with no music and formal, almost Elizabethan, language; a chanted Eucharist with traditional music and more contemporary language; a spoken Eucharist with traditional music and more contemporary language; a spoken Eucharist with contemporary music, a children's sermon, and even more contemporary language; another spoken Eucharist with contemporary music and more contemporary language; a Eucharist with folk music for and with our homeless neighbors; and, at day's end, a concluding service of sung Compline in a darkened sanctuary. Other Episcopal churches offer other variations on worship style, so that you might find everything from incense, candles, and Bach to blue jeans, clapping, and rock.

Presiding Bishop Jefferts Schori says she has experienced transcendent experiences in many worship settings,

> experiences of being drawn outside myself, into a sense of union with the cosmos, into greater compassion, into solidarity with those present in body as well as the communion of saints and with humanity and all creation. Those occasions have come in varied worship environments—from great cathedrals with complex music and liturgy, to the earnest and dignified simplicity of indigenous worship in the great outdoors. Each has something to do with authenticity expressed in context, when liturgy and preaching partake of the local and encourage transcendence.

For Rowan Williams, the same question about powerful worship experiences causes him to think not only of his first Anglican service, but of "many more memories from my time as Archbishop. Celebrating at the graves of recent martyrs in the Solomon Islands, in the sports stadium in

Harare with thousands of Christians who had experienced persecution from government there. The cathedral in New York the day after 9/11. The chapel of the Sisters of the Sacred Cross in rural Wales on a winter evening."

Our connection with other worshippers, with the larger Church (past and present, as Bishop Jefferts Schori notes), and with God, comes in many Episcopal and Anglican settings of worship, in many places, accompanied by many kinds of music or without music. What underlies all of these experiences, though—what makes them Anglican or Episcopalian—is their use of the prayer book liturgy. Again, we find the Book of Common Prayer at the very heart of all we do.

Of course, almost all religious observances are liturgical. Many religious traditions claim to be non-liturgical. This claim is generally untrue. It may be that a church doesn't have a book of prayers from which worship is drawn or a set of words that are required to be spoken every Sunday, but we human beings are creatures of pattern and habit. Few churches are making things up anew every time they come together for corporate worship—and few worshippers would find comfort in a routine that was no routine at all. So virtually every church offers a common sequence of worship, and most offer familiar words, phrases, and blessings, even if they think of themselves as nonliturgical.

One of my most cherished memories from the tradition in which I was raised was the choir's weekly benediction at Pritchard Memorial Baptist Church in Charlotte, North Carolina: "The Lord bless you and keep you / The Lord make his face to shine upon you / And be gracious unto you / Amen." That congregation would have reacted with shock had someone suggested that they "had" to include that blessing every Sunday. But they also would have reacted strongly had someone suggested that the routine be changed.

Repetition and pattern are human comforts, and they surround us in our daily lives, whether or not we realize it. Every morning when the ladies of *The View* begin their familiar banter; every night, when Jon Stewart looks up from marking up his copy to announce, "Hey, welcome to *The Daily Show*, my name is Jon Stewart"; every Sunday evening when the cantering theme to *A Game of Thrones* accompanies the familiar unfolding panorama of Westeros, we are reassured by patterns.

Pattern places some borders around our lives and some limits on the chaos around us.

That comforting repetition is made official in the worship of the Episcopal Church because of the liturgical tradition we inherited from the Catholic Mass. Every Sunday, with only minor variations because of season and focus, we give ourselves to the communal worship of God through liturgy we have grown to love, through words that open us up to each other and to ourselves, as well as to the Divine.

Kirk Royal, a lay leader at St. Philip's Episcopal Church in Durham, North Carolina, reflects on how Episcopal worship has become central to his understanding of who he is and where he's come from:

> It's the constancy of the liturgy itself that I adore most. When I've descended into the darkest of places mentally and perhaps even spiritually, it was the liturgy that remained fixed and allowed me to still be able to pray even when I thought I didn't have it in me to do so. Likewise, now that I'm living more fully and abundantly than I can ever recall, the liturgy is still here . . . only now, rather than being a cast holding my broken soul together, it exists as the conduit by which that now healed yet forever fragile soul tells out the greatness of the Lord.

Like my childhood memory of choral benediction, many words and phrases from the Episcopal liturgy bring me comfort and inspire me to think of God as present and powerful. I still get a chill during the recitation of the Nicene Creed when we say of Jesus, "And his kingdom will have no end." I don't know what that means exactly; I struggle, as many do, with the question of the afterlife and what God has intended for us next. But to imagine whatever it is that Jesus—our brother and companion on the way—is going to be in charge of makes this a beautiful and comforting phrase.

I am a huge fan of the Ash Wednesday service, and in particular, the painful and true phrase spoken as the ashes are drawn in a cross upon my forehead: "Remember that you are dust, and to dust you shall return."

During the latter part of the Eucharistic Prayer, at the close of the blessing of the elements of communion, the priest will often raise (or instruct the others at the altar to raise) the consecrated bread and wine and say to the gathered worshippers: "The Gifts of God for the People of God." And if she or he doesn't repeat this next bit (the prayer book calls them optional; for me they seem to have become essential!), I will often say it under my breath, to the great amusement of my son Chandler: "Take them in remembrance that Christ died for you, and feed on him in your hearts by faith, with thanksgiving."

Just typing those words brings tears to my eyes; clearly I have powerful emotional and spiritual associations with those words—and with the act of communion that follows. And I'm certainly not the only one who finds words and liturgical acts triggering closeness to God and the community of which I'm a part. Ambrose of Milan, the spiritual father of Augustine of Hippo, said, "You have shown yourself to me, O Christ, face to face. I have met you in your sacraments." Terri Morgan, a lay leader in the Diocese of Texas, told me, "Our liturgy makes God present, in the liturgy of the Word and the liturgy of the Eucharist."

Erin Warde also singles out the Eucharist as a place where we meet Jesus:

> The first time I ever took Eucharist, when I went back to the pew I could still feel the burn of the wine, and it felt like Christ had met me at the altar and decided to walk with me the rest of the way. I had always struggled with feeling like I knew Christ was present with me, but I couldn't feel Christ's presence. *That* felt like Christ's presence. I think it was also a large part of my calling to the priesthood; I want to invite others to feel Christ's presence.

In worship we are meeting more than our fellow congregants; we are meeting Christ face to face. The liturgy of beautiful words and significant symbols builds part of the bridge between us. Our communal participation, our prayers and gestures, builds the rest. When we find a church and a tradition that resonates with our own emotional and spiritual makeup, we meet God in that place with the people around us. Sometimes we don't know we've found such a tradition until we blunder into it—I didn't know how much I would love Episcopal liturgy until I gave myself up to it week after week. And lots of people with whom I interact don't know what I'm talking about—until they experience it too.

Rowan Williams argues, "When we read the Bible and celebrate the sacraments, what we are doing is repeatedly coming out of the shadows, back to where truth lives, where Jesus lives. . . . We don't learn the truth as isolated individuals, any more than we grow and discover as isolated individuals."[14] Worship sustains and nourishes fellowship; it tears down walls; it heals old divisions; it creates new communities; and it recreates us in the process.

My experience of liturgy changed lots of things about me, and Episcopal worship has changed others too. Sara Milcs, a progressive lesbian journalist who had always scorned religion, experienced her first Eucharist at age forty-six and discovered to her surprise and possibly even her dismay that it rocked her world. "Holy communion knocked me upside down and forced me to deal with the impossible reality of God," Miles writes in her best-selling spiritual autobiography, *Take This Bread*.[15]

The experience of sacramental and liturgical worship can startle even people who are devoutly Christian. I mentioned earlier in the book that in January I colead a weeklong retreat for Baptist pastors and seminarians through Baylor's Truett Seminary. While some Baptist churches have embraced formal liturgy, many remain determinedly informal, and many Baptists do not regularly celebrate the Lord's Supper, as the Eucharist is sometimes called in Protestant circles.

During our week together, I introduce many of these pastors and seminarians to liturgical worship. We use written liturgy for morning and evening prayer, and that modified Book of Common Prayer communion for our final act of worship together. Part of my task is to show them the most beautiful language of praise and worship human beings have created. We use the Psalms at every service, of course, and like N. T. Wright, I believe that the Psalms must be central to Christian worship. But I also want my students to hear the collects, repeat the responses, and learn or relearn how God speaks to us in repeated prayers in the variety of circumstances such as Kirk Royal described—the underlying philosophy and beauty of liturgy.

Early in the week, my Baptist friends sometimes grumble about the repetition of chants and prayers. They are used to a more extemporaneous type of prayer. But during the week of our worship together, many of them begin to feel the pull of liturgy. They begin to sing the chants with some gusto, to speak the responses as though they matter. And by the time we reach the end-of-the-week Eucharist, something transformational has happened. These die-hard Baptist pastors and pastors-in-training often have tears in their eyes as they take the bread and the wine.

"It's a tangible expression of what they talk about all the time," says Hulitt Gloer, the Truett Seminary professor with whom I do the retreat. "Of everything they believe. They've just not used to *saying* it. To *doing* it."

That's what liturgy does, and why Episcopalians treasure it: It brings Christian faith and practice alive. As my friend and seminary professor the Reverend Bill Adams used to advise, you have to stand back and let the liturgy do its work. Liturgy is love, grace, forgiveness, community, and resurrection poured into prayers and actions and symbols. Liturgy is a ceremony, a play, a story we act out together in community. And liturgy is filled with beauty that grows within us and draws us toward God, the source of all Beauty. Whatever else we may be as a Church, our foundation is common worship that directs us to do all the other things we are called to do in the rest of the week, and offers us comfort, insight, and strength for the journey.

Questions for Discussion

1. What is the most powerful experience of communal worship you can recall—if you can recall one? Can you remember a time when you were part of a worshipping community and didn't feel at all connected to what was happening?
2. What patterns, repetitions, or phrases are meaningful ones for you in your daily life? If you have ever been involved in worship, what liturgy has been life-giving for you?
3. At what times in your life do you remember feeling that you were part of a community? What were the elements that helped make you feel included?

For Further Reading

Susan J. White, *The Spirit of Worship: The Liturgical Tradition* (Maryknoll, NY: Orbis, 1999).

The former professor of worship at Brite Divinity School, White explores what the Church has understood about liturgy across the past two millennia, and describes how liturgy both lets us see who and where we are and helps to create community.

Rowan Williams, *Being Christian* (Grand Rapids, MI: William B. Eerdmans, 2014).

In this short but beautifully argued book, Lord Williams argues for the four essential elements of being Christian—all of which (baptism, Bible, Eucharist, and prayer) have strong and sometimes essential connections to our life of corporate worship.

N. T. Wright, *Simply Christian: Why Christianity Makes Sense* (New York: HarperOne, 2010).

The former bishop of Durham and prolific New Testament scholar offers this popular book on Anglican/Episcopal faith and practice. The views of God, Christian community, worship, prayer, and social justice he details here grow out of his lifetime of faith and service to the Church.

Beauty and the Life of God: Music, Culture, and the Incarnate Way

As I write the first draft of this chapter this morning, I am working at a creekside cabin in the Texas Hill Country. Miles away, at St. Peter's Episcopal Church in Kerrville, congregants are singing, praying, receiving the Eucharist and their priest's blessing and benediction. Here, birds are chirping in the trees and bees are flitting in the bushes. A hummingbird just turbo-buzzed me, the sun is reflecting off the clear water, and I am surrounded by natural beauty. It's one of those moments that just about anyone could recognize as blessed—as a moment filled with light, or spirit, or God, if you believe in such a thing, which of course I do.

Psalm 19 tells us "The heavens are telling the glory of God, and the firmament proclaims his handiwork," and American culture is full of people who seek and seize these moments of natural declaration. They include the people Lillian Daniel writes about who are militantly spiritual but not religious who seem to believe that religious people don't *get* that God might be speaking through hummingbirds or sunlight or the wind on the waters. It's true that some American Christians limit their revelation of God to scripture —or to revelations of the Holy Spirit. But Episcopalians are certainly among the religious people who do experience God in this way. Part of being spiritual and religious is believing we live in a world created by God and filled with God—what we call a truly incarnational theology. As the Celtic tradition teaches us, "Matter matters," and God entering into the world in the human form of Jesus is not the only incarnation we celebrate. It's simply the most important.

Although Episcopalians experience the Divine in the breaking of the bread, we also understand that God is moving in the world outside the walls of our churches, that God is still revealing God's self daily, and so we pay attention to what is happening in the created world, as well as how God might be moving in human creation. The Reverend Roger Joslin, a priest from Bentonville, Arkansas, wrote a great book about the spiritual value of running. Rowan Williams has written books seeking the beauty and meaning in Dostoevsky, Flannery O'Connor, C. S. Lewis, and the Welsh artist and poet David Jones. I've written books about how we can find and explore theology in movies and Harry Potter and superhero stories and the music of U2. The Reverend Bill Miller, a priest from the Hawaiian island of Kauai, has written a recent book centering on spirituality and beer, and the Lord knows I have experienced more than a few moments of revelation with priests and bishops over a beer or two.

Some religious people might be (okay: are) scandalized by the idea that God might be moving in the bubbles of a good pale ale or in the pounding beat of a Bruce Springsteen anthem. But one of the first areas of connection I found with Episcopal life was its recognition that if God is the author of Truth and Beauty, then those things in this life that are true and beautiful point us back to their source. Full disclosure: This is a belief that goes back to the early Church Fathers; look at the opening of Augustine's *Confessions*, "Late have I loved you, beauty so old and so new." Wherever we find them in this life, truth and beauty are signs of the larger Sign, smaller pieces of love, grace, and light that remind us of the love, grace, and light that emanate from God.

So maybe it's not so odd that even when I was far from knowing God through worship and a faith community, I felt I was experiencing the presence of God in movies and music and other created beauty. As I mentioned earlier, *Pulp Fiction* was a film that had a powerful effect on me during some of the most difficult times of my life, and it is far from alone among works of art in the spiritual power it manifests. We can (and should) talk about music and plays and books and other films and all sorts of human creations that mediate the Divine for us in some way—and that is, in fact, the point of this chapter, to consciously explore how Episcopalians experience and are affected by art, culture, and the created world.

Part of our love of beauty obviously comes from our Catholic heritage. Our beautiful liturgy, as we've already noted, was one of the elements of Catholic (and Orthodox) worship we wanted to keep. Our classically beautiful churches and cathedrals owe much to the medieval cathedrals of France and Germany and Italy—and England. Westminster Abbey, Canterbury Cathedral, Salisbury Cathedral, and Chester Cathedral were all built before the Protestant Reformation. Those twelfth-century panels of stained glass from Canterbury that recently toured the Metropolitan Museum of Art and the Getty Museum were originally created to look down on the tomb of the martyr Thomas Becket. They had a teaching function, of course, to allow illiterate parishioners to understand something about the biblical ancestors of Jesus (and that Christians are a part of a longer history with greater legitimacy than any secular ruler). But they were also intended to awe viewers with their jewel-like beauty, with the way they colored the light that flowed in from above.

A few centuries later, Protestant reformers in England broke windows, stripped jewels from the cathedral shrines, and destroyed the shrines themselves. They also shattered or removed altars and statues from Canterbury and many other cathedrals. Many Protestant churches to this day are marvels of simplicity. Some might call them spare, sparse, even severe in their lack of art and ornament. The Protestant reformers were suspicious of art and decoration because they considered it idolatrous, and believed it represented Catholic excess. But although we think of ourselves as Protestant, we in the Anglican/Episcopal tradition remain Catholic in our love of beautiful things.

Many of us believe that we worship through each of our senses as well as through heart and head. It is one of the reasons why the sermon is not the primary focus of Episcopal worship as it is in most Protestant churches. Some Episcopalians revel in fragrant flowers, fine linen, sparkling brass and silver, rich incense, flickering candles, and awe-inspiring organ music. Unlike plain and functional worship spaces, our sanctuaries often include statues, paintings, beautiful chalices and patens for communion, brass candlesticks, jeweled crosses, and, yes, lots of stained glass.

I've spent a lot of time looking at the stained glass at St. David's in Austin. While our glass is certainly less ancient than that of Canterbury—the older windows date from the church's founding in the mid-nineteenth century—they seem no less beautiful to me, and they put me in just as holy a place when I sit and meditate upon them. The large window on the south (where a rose window might be in a cathedral) depicts David of Wales, our patron saint, in hues of green and gold. Windows on the east and west walls of the nave commemorate faithful parishioners, or reproduce scenes from the scriptures. But it's far from the only art to be found in our sanctuary. Our high altar features a triptych—a three-part painting common in medieval religious art—which is a really fine reproduction of a fifteenth-century altarpiece by Perugino. (The original, *Three Panels from an Altarpiece, Certosa*, resides in the National Gallery in London.) The wider central painting depicts the Madonna and Child with an angel; the archangels Raphael and Michael occupy the right and left frames, respectively. I often sit and admire the altarpiece when I am seated at the altar to serve communion.

Why do we have so many beautiful things in our worship space? This Perugino reproduction feels like an extravagance in a historic sanctuary already saturated with beauty. Many parishioners never even note the painting, any more than they could describe all the stained glass windows surrounding them every Sunday. (Some could, though; after I asked a question about one of the windows in a recent sermon, several parishioners stopped on their way out to tell me they'd been puzzling over that window their whole lives!) Most parishioners probably couldn't tell you that the altar is made of Italian marble, although they would probably describe it as white, gleaming, and gorgeous. Most couldn't tell you where the colorful banner next to the pulpit depicting St. David came from (I know that —the Reverend Chad Vaughn, now serving in Atlanta, designed and ordered it). Most of us couldn't detail for you the woodcarvings in the choir or the altar rail, nor could we tell you about the brass statue supporting the lectern on the epistle side (it's an eagle), nor could we do much more than tell you that the elaborate raised wooden pulpit built in 1869 is tall and very imposing. (And it is; I feel like I've climbed up into a crow's nest on a sailing ship when I preach there.) And that's not to say anything about the flowers at the altar, or the towering candles, or the shimmering vestments worn by the clergy, or the crisp starched fine linens covering the altar, or—

Again, why so many beautiful things? Aren't these a distraction? An affectation? Shouldn't worshippers be paying close attention to the scripture readings, the sermon, the words of the liturgy instead of letting their eyes wander? Aren't there (I feel myself channeling the voices of Protestant reformers) better things on which a church could be using its resources? Why so many beautiful things?

Well, with all respect to our Protestant brothers and sisters and to any Episcopalians consciously worshipping in simple spaces, I can suggest several good reasons. We are first, as Torey Lightcap, priest from Nebraska, briefly notes, "giving our best back to God." God is the object of our worship; we are the worshippers. Stacy Walker-Frontjes, priest from Illinois, explains: "In worship we are reflecting the beauty, light, and peace of God, no matter how pale and shadowy that image may be in this world. And we give it our best for Jesus—the Holy Incarnate One—who loves us more than we can imagine each and every day." When we worship God, we want to create a beautiful experience, something that honors the One who has surrounded us with beauty.

Second, the beauty helps us to connect to the God we worship through more than the beautiful words of the liturgy. The Reverend Doug Earle, a priest from San Antonio, argues, "Words can get us only so far." As Rebecca Massingill Raulerson, a layperson from Alabama (and better half of the Reverend Aaron Raulerson) notes, "God created me with five senses and I like to use them all when I worship." A rich worship experience might contain multiple visual textures, the smell of incense, the sounds of Bach or Ralph Vaughn Williams, the kinetic impressions from kneeling, standing, sitting, bowing, and, of course, the taste of bread and wine before we are finished.

Why do we revel in beauty? Carol Brown, a layperson from Bastrop, Texas, says it is for "the same reason you and your bride chose a beautiful location and your finest clothes to get married"—to honor a beautiful occasion by surrounding it with the best you can offer, so that there is "something reverential, sacramental, special and holy about that kind of beauty reserved for a certain event." My wife, Jeanie, speaks of the sense that you are walking into someplace special when you enter a beautified worship space.

Both responses help us understand a third reason beauty matters. Not only does it demonstrate our reverence for God, not only does it help us to worship God through all our senses, but a beautiful place to worship helps us to mark off a particular space and time as sacramental. We live in a fast-paced world surrounded by many distractions; when we can enter into a place that fills us with a sense of beauty, wonder, and peace, it bounces us out of our usual ways of being. We feel that God is with us as we seek to be with God. It offers, as Greg Rickel wrote in the Foreword, a place where people can connect with More.

Finally, beautiful spaces for worship are even linked to the question of social justice. Everett Lees, priest from Tulsa, reminded me about the Anglo-Catholic priests associated with the Oxford Movement in the nine-teenth century who wanted to bring more beauty into the lives of their parishioners, many of whom lived in slums. Bishop Andy Doyle, too, talked to me about this idea, describing his father, who was an

> "old school high churchman." What I mean by that is my father loved the beauty and richness of the liturgy with all of its art, poetry, and music. I saw liturgy as an almost baroque combination of art for the senses. . . . But my father believed this beauty was ultimately so that people could be drawn in toward God, and that this beauty was most of all for the poor, the day laborer, the paycheck-to-paycheck family; for them, this beauty was transformational.

This final reason for beauty in our churches seems particularly rel-evant for any church, serving, as mine does, a downtown neighborhood filled with the poor and the homeless. Many of our neighbors are sleep-ing rough and haunting the food banks. They cannot afford a Starbucks latte with a heart design drawn on its surface, or any of the other minor beauties we take for granted in the course of our everyday lives. But in every worship service in our historic sanctuary I see one or more of our homeless neighbors taking in the sights, the sounds, the rich taste of port on their tongues, and being reminded that the world is filled with beauty, a witness that God is beautiful.

St. David's is one single Episcopal church, and not the biggest nor the wealthiest nor the oldest. I don't mention the beautiful items in my church to brag—or at least, not merely to brag. I talked you through our sanctuary because St. David's represents all those churches from the Anglican tradition in which worshippers have carried their love of beauty inside the church, committed their resources to surround themselves with works of art. They felt closer to God surrounded by beauty—and they felt they were in some way honoring God through gathering this beauty. And whether or not they understood this theologically or simply intuitively, they were honoring creation and their fellow creatures through these human creations.

The love of beauty is a theology hard at work in Episcopal life. The Right Reverend Richard Harries, formerly the bishop of Oxford, notes "it is central to Christianity, properly understood, that there is a resemblance, a relationship, between the beauty we experience in nature, in the arts, in a genuinely good person, and in God; and that which tantalizes, beckons and calls us in beauty has its origin in God himself."[16] Episcopalians are open to beauty from a lot of directions, and are often ardent consumers of the arts: They read, they watch movies and TV, they listen to music, and in all of this they differ from some Christians by being willing to consider challenging art that some Christians would condemn, because they find God moving in the deep.

To judge from my Facebook feed, a lot of Episcopalians are watching or have watched *Mad Men*, *Game of Thrones*, *Breaking Bad*, *Downton Abbey*, and *House of Cards*, despite the fact that these shows don't depict good Christians doing good Christian things. In fact, many of them feature antiheroes who are rewarded for bad behavior, and good characters who die or are damaged by their attempts to do the right thing. And yet, the shows themselves are thoughtfully written and stylishly filmed, and their attempts to wrestle with the paradoxes of human life have a dark beauty of their own.

Some moralists insist that Christians should consume only works of art that reinforce their beliefs. Episcopalians do not generally think this way—or at least think of our "beliefs" as so limited. We understand that any work of art that tells the truth is doing a service. These works of art seem to be telling some hard truths about life. Bad people often prosper (is Kevin Spacey's Frank Underwood on *House of Cards* really that different from many powerful and manipulative men who have run our country?) and good people often suffer (in almost any episode of *Game of Thrones* or *Downton Abbey*), and art that pretends otherwise isn't telling the truth. Some of our greatest Christian writers have written depressing and down-beat stories. Flannery O'Connor's work, for example, is famously diffi-cult, and filled with racism, hatred, small-mindedness, and chaos. Rowan Williams deftly explains what this lifelong Catholic was up to. She was "a robust defender of orthodox doctrine and traditional devotion, as well as being a scathing critic of religious subculture. Some of her most pun-gent observations are to do with assumptions about 'Catholic art' that insist that such art should be edifying and moral; this, she argues, plays straight into the hands of critics of the Church who hold that dogmatic belief incapacitates a creative writer."[17]

O'Connor's stories, often violent, always disturbing, revolve around a moment of grace, often small, sometimes hidden, but always present. In her work—and in the fiction of the Anglican mystery writer P. D. James (whom Lord Williams once described to me as "our greatest Neo-Augustinian"), we are brought face to face with the distasteful truth of human life, that it is often violent, short, and brutish—but that it is also graced by the possibility of some beauty, wonder, and connection to God.

As consumers of culture, we too should look for beauty and truth, and we should consume with some discretion. While I read, teach, and write about literature and culture, there are some works that I recognize as not being good for my soul. I stopped watching *Mad Men* and *Breaking Bad* because I couldn't find a point of light to which I could attach myself. I stopped watching *The Walking Dead* because I couldn't bear the loss of one beloved character after another. I had to fast-forward a number of scenes in the movie *The Girl with the Dragon Tattoo* and avert my eyes from the beautifully-shot, Cannes-selected German movie *Nothing Bad Can Happen* because their intense violence and degradation felt soul-killing, and so (for me, at least) it probably was.

I would be the last to judge anyone else who learned something from these works. For me, consuming them was a poor choice. I've often been on the other side of the question. Over the years, people have questioned my championing of *Pulp Fiction* or the Bourne films or *No Country for Old Men*, which were for various reasons disturbing to them. I get it. Sometimes what is beautiful to you isn't beautiful to me, and vice versa. I can say that in each of these works, I felt I was learning something true and necessary, or being reminded about the realities of grace and justice as I understand them through my faith. My own spiritual journey is a reminder that these works from outside our tradition (nobody is trying to claim Quentin Tarantino as a closet Episcopalian) can still teach and inspire us. Justin Martyr, writing in the first century BCE, argued that God draws people to God through the created order, and such creations— even though they're not anointed as "Christian"—can be a part of our journey as well.

Among those artists we think of as somehow Christian who con- sciously deal with issues of faith, forgiveness, grace, sin, justice, and redemption, we might find an even greater span of revelation. We could consider *The Tree of Life* (2011), a challenging and meditative film by the Episcopalian writer/director Terrence Malick. (I call Mr. Malick Episcopalian because he attended St. Stephen's Episcopal School in Austin and still reportedly attends a local Episcopal church. Since he is famously reclusive, all I know for certain about him is that his wife Ecky graduated from my seminary, and that he chose my friend the Reverend Kelly Koonce to play Father Haynes in *Tree of Life*.) His movie wrestles with life, death, God, and what everything means—if, in fact it means anything. (The movie suggests it does.)

At the film's opening, Mrs. O'Brien (Jessica Chastain) says that there are two ways through life, the way of nature and the way of grace. One wants to please itself, one offers love and forgiveness, and she decides, "The only way to be happy is to love. Unless you love, your life will flash by." Later in the movie, her husband, played by Brad Pitt, laments his choices in a way that sounds Episcopalian in its regard for beauty: "I wanted to be loved because I was great; a big man. I'm nothing. Look at the glory around us; trees, birds. I lived in shame. I dishonored it all, and didn't notice the glory. I'm a foolish man."

The Tree of Life is not a thriller (Roger Ebert, who proposed the film be listed as one of the all-time greats, described it as a prayer, which helped me to understand it, finally), so its plot is not its primary reason for being. What happens to the individual characters is less important than what the movie concludes about life, so I don't believe I am offering spoilers by telling you that the movie's end seems to offer some possible version of how, in whatever the life to come might be, we will encounter those we have loved and lost and be reconciled with even those who did us harm. It's a deeply spiritual—some would say "religious"—film, and, like O'Connor, as far from simple verities and pieties as one can get. With Malick, whose films are famously both beautiful and opaque, one of the points seems to be the experience of cinema. After I had thought (a lot) about *The Tree of Life*, I realized that it was indeed an experience like entering into a beautiful church.

The renowned writer and preacher the Reverend Barbara Brown Taylor is another great Episcopal artist who has brought her faith to the work she has tried to create in truth and beauty. Taylor was chosen by Baylor University as one of the ten greatest preachers in the English language, and while this was certainly a subjective designation, it drew the attention of people around the world to her exquisite sermons. (I still recall one of her sermons delivered in our seminary on a gospel text so difficult it isn't even included in the lectionary for Sundays. It was nonetheless one of the five greatest sermons I've heard in my life.)

Taylor, who is a poet and fiction writer as well as writer of sermons and memoir, says that early in her life as a priest, she learned that truth and beauty were to be her tools at least as much as theological reflection; that in fact, they were a vital form of theological reflection. In *An Altar in the World*, she tells this story:

> Many years ago now, a wise old priest invited me to come speak at his church in Alabama. "What do you want me to talk about?" I asked him.
>
> "Come tell us what is saving your life now," he answered. It was as if he had swept his arm across a dusty table and brushed all the formal china to the ground. I did not have to try to say correct things that were true for everyone. I did not have to use theological language that conformed to the historical teachings of the church. All I had to do was figure out how I stayed as close to that reality as I could, and then find some way to talk about it that helped my listeners figure out those same things for themselves.[18]

Great artists are offering us a chance to wrestle with our own questions through the art they offer us; that—and to be true and beautiful—are two of the primary functions of art.

I'd like to close this section with some thoughts about a rock band. Although they aren't Episcopalians, I've written and spoken about, preached on, and played the music of U2 for years now, and in the words, music, and lives of these musicians many think of as the greatest rock band since the Beatles, we can see many of the lessons from our tradition about incarnation coming to life.

First, I think it's important to note that although I'll be speaking of U2 in the realm of Christian artists, it's a little more complicated than that. Three of the four members of U2 identify themselves as Christian (the fourth, bassist Adam Clayton, is sometimes described by his bandmates as the most Christian of them all), and some of their music clearly draws from the Christian tradition ("40" is a musical setting of Psalm 40 with the chorus drawn from Psalm 60, while "Gloria" is a contemporary setting of "Glory to God in the highest," an integral part of our liturgy), but some years ago, the band members were faced with the decision about whether they were going to be a "Christian band" or a rock band. They were thrown out of their faith community for choosing to continue playing rock music, but the results were tangible. By choosing to make beautiful music, not to advance an agenda through their music, they have spoken to many more people than they ever could have reached through making Christian music.

Every U2 album has seen them recording songs like "Pride (in the Name of Love)," "Beautiful Day," "City of Blinding Lights," and "New Year's Day," songs that deal with matters both spiritual and temporal. What does it mean to live a life filled with compassion and justice? What are the temptations this world throws at us? Every U2 concert ever given has been a gathering of people from all parts of society, a powerful emotional and spiritual experience that many people have likened to worship.

What links U2 to our tradition besides this Episcopalian's love for them (and my sitting down to tea at St. Pancras Station in London one day with the Anglican priest who serves as their chaplain)? Well, Episcopalians Sarah Dylan Breuer and the Reverend Paige Blair

respectively created and popularized a worship service called the
"U2charist"—a service of communion that employs U2's music as hymns
and service music, and it became an international sensation. I've participated in U2charists both as preacher and as musician. When these
beautiful and topical songs are combined with our liturgy, something
happens that is greater than the sum of its two sizable parts. U2's music
has a profound effect on people, and that effect gets magnified by the
beauty and framework of liturgy. And how cool is it that Episcopalians
thought to combine them like this?

U2's music is not the only popular music used in Episcopal services, by
the way. I myself have accompanied Eucharists with the music of Johnny
Cash, Hank Williams, and the Beatles, and the Reverend Bill Miller has
developed jazz masses for the churches he has served in Austin, Houston,
and Hawaii. For him, that pairing of jazz with the liturgy was a natural
evolution of his life and faith:

> I grew up in Houston which, believe it or not, has a rich jazz and
> blues tradition—it's closer to Louisiana than to San Antonio! So
> early on, I was exposed to some of the greats such as Arnett Cobb,
> Milton Larkin, and Sam "Lightnin' Hopkins." My dad was an elder
> in our fundamentalist Church of Christ (no instruments but we sho
> could sang!) and he'd take me on Sunday afternoons to an African
> American mission church we supported. I grew quite comfortable in
> other contexts and other cultures and learned appreciation.
>
> When I got to St. James' in Austin, I found myself in a historically
> African American context but wanted to do something the African
> American Missionary Baptist Church next door was *not* doing, reach
> a different audience. They already had the corner on the gospel mar-
> ket. But no one was doing jazz. It made all the sense in the world
> for us to start a jazz festival with a Jazz Mass. We had many jazz afi-
> cionados in the congregation. I was surprised to discover that Duke
> Ellington's three Sacred Concerts were all premiered in Episcopal or
> Anglican houses of worship, and no one was really performing any
> of this music (which Ellington called "the most important work" he
> had composed or performed). I began to collaborate with jazz musi-
> cians to create Jazz Masses (collaboration is as important as creativ-
> ity!) and the rest is history.

Bill also owns a bar and music venue, Padre's, in Marfa, Texas, and he sees Padre's as an extension of his life as a priest. "We wanted it to be a place where people who are different from one another could come together and break bread and drink wine (or beer) and praise God (or at least tap their toes)," he says.

For Bill—and for many of my Episcopal and Anglican friends—music is a vital part of who we are. The Reverend Tim Ditchfield, chaplain at King's College, London, tells me that his early memories of dancing to the music of the British rock/electronic band New Order are among his most joyful. I myself have joyful memories of sitting on the front porch of my seminary classmate (now the Reverend) Joe Behen listening to music. Each of us would take turns playing a track that had been important to us—and then saying something about why it mattered to us.

In our love for great art, music, movies, and other forms of created beauty, what we're doing is acknowledging that there's really no line between the sacred and secular. All of creation can be sacramental. Episcopalians resist drawing artificial distinctions between what is holy and what is not. All of us can probably remember a moment in our lives when God spoke to us out of the last place we might have expected it. A lovely moment in the movie *American Beauty* (1999) both illustrates and helps explain this phenomenon. The quirky videographer, Ricky (Wes Bentley), talks about seeing—and filming—a plastic bag blowing in the wind. We see his footage; the bag, dancing and twirling, truly is a magical image. But what helps make the scene sacramental is the combination of image and words, as Ricky describes what he filmed:

> This bag was just dancing with me. Like a little kid begging me to play with it. For fifteen minutes. That's the day I realized that there was this entire life behind things, and this incredibly benevolent force that wanted me to know there was no reason to be afraid, ever. . . . Sometimes there's so much beauty in the world.[19]

There is so much beauty in the world, and the Episcopal tradition calls for us to mark it as holy. One of my favorite prayers from the prayer book, "For Vocation in Daily Work," makes this clear in its opening: "Almighty God, our Heavenly Father, you declare your glory and show forth your handiwork in the heavens and in the earth." We see God's glory in our churches, in beautiful sanctuaries and wonderful music, but we should also see it everywhere else, if our eyes are open. In a world created by God and imbued with God's creative force, *American Beauty* suggests that even the garbage can sing of God's presence. Part of being Episcopalian, of being both religious and spiritual, is being present and available to God's presence, wherever we may find it. Every day we are surrounded in countless ways by the glory of God, and we can—and should—give thanks for that.

Questions for Discussion

1. How has God spoken to you outside the bounds of traditional religion? What made you think it was God speaking?
2. Who are some of your favorite musicians and composers? In what ways do they speak to you?
3. What stories have been important in your spiritual development? What movies, TV shows, and books do you return to over and over? Why?

For Further Reading

Garrett, Greg. *We Get to Carry Each Other: The Gospel according to U2* (Louisville: Westminster John Knox Press, 2009).

In this work, I explore the music and lives of the Irish rock band U2, and suggest the lessons on compassion, justice, and community they offer, as well as why we ought to pay serious attention to art and music as revelation from God.

Thomas Harries, *Art and the Beauty of God* (1993; New York: Continuum, 2005).

One of the most beautiful and accessible books I've read on the field of theological aesthetics, how we understand God through beauty and human art. Bishop Harries gathers the treasures of the Christian tradition in building a strong case for beauty as a central part of our faith and practice.

Taylor, Barbara Brown. *An Altar in the World: A Geography of Faith* (New York: HarperOne, 2009).

The Reverend Taylor offers us well-crafted stories and suggests a multitude of spiritual disciplines to allow us to see the holy in the world around us, beginning with the necessary tasks of waking up to God and paying attention.

Williams, Rowan. *Grace and Necessity: Reflections on Art and Love* (Harrisburg, PA: Morehouse, 2005).

Using the work of Welsh artist/poet David Jones and the American fiction writer Flannery O'Connor to illustrate his points, the former archbishop of Canterbury discusses one of his favorite topics, the relationship between Christian faith and practice and the arts.

Living Together: How the Culture Wars Almost Killed Us— But Made Us Stronger

On June 2, 2014, the Reverend Stacey Walker-Frontjes posted an invitation on Facebook for people to be married at her church, St. Paul's Episcopal in Dekalb, Illinois. This in itself would not have been particularly notable. Churches do tend to host weddings, and June is traditionally a month filled with them. But the opening of her invitation was: "On the first day ALL couples can obtain a wedding license in Illinois, I'm sharing this link to my church's website about weddings." And on that webpage about marriages and blessings at St. Paul's, you could see three images: the hands of a bride and groom, two women smiling and holding white flowers, and a rainbow pride flag.

I went to seminary with Stacey. She was my next-door neighbor. She is neither a radical nor an anarchist. She is a mom and a wife and a compassionate and hard-working priest. She is not pushing a "homosexual agenda" or trying to destroy the Church from within or acting as a secret tool of Satan, although some of our Christian brothers and sisters have seen support for gays and lesbians in the Church as treason or blasphemy.

While some Christian denominations continue to call gays sinful and to exclude them from their ranks, Stacey is right in the mainstream of the Episcopal Church, which has decided, after painful but necessary conflict, that God's grace cannot be denied to any of God's children. What are the practical implications of this decision? Gays and lesbians should be welcome in our pews and in our leadership positions. Gays and lesbians seeking blessing on their lifelong relationships should feel as welcome in the Episcopal Church as straight couples. What Stacey was saying in her post was that if the law of the land permits people to get married—and Illinois now does—then the Episcopal Church should be a place where all are made to feel welcome and loved.

Since the Right Reverend Gene Robinson, a gay priest living in a long-term relationship, was elected as bishop of New Hampshire and ratified by the Episcopal General Convention in 2003, human sexuality has dominated conversation about the Episcopal Church and about the future of the Anglican Communion. After the General Convention's vote, Episcopalians who did not believe gay Christians should be included in the full life of the Church began to peel away, and national Anglican churches (particularly those in Africa, where homosexuality remains a huge cultural taboo) began to distance themselves from the Episcopal Church—and, slowly, from the Anglican Communion itself as a communal body.

During this process, not only were the relationships between the Episcopal Church and other churches in the Communion damaged, but hundreds of American parishes, including some of the denomination's largest and wealthiest, withdrew from the national Church, taking their members and their resources with them. Average Sunday Attendance, a measurement of involvement used by the Episcopal Church, declined by 10 percent between 2002 and 2012, and while we've considered some of the societal trends that might have contributed to lower involvement, many also attribute a large part of that decline to the ongoing conflict over human sexuality.

The Episcopal Church's crisis over human sexuality—and again I am using "crisis" as a moment of both potential disaster and opportunity—shaped the Church and its practice for a decade, and while the debate has had what I and many consider a positive and hopeful outcome—the 2012 decision by the national Church to permit same-sex blessings, bishops permitting—no one would deny that the struggle led to bitterness and fierce divisions among people who professed to believe in Christian unity. Certainly one of the people closest to the action was Presiding Bishop Katharine Jefferts Schori, who reflects that for her:

The saddest part has been our internal focus in the midst of this wrestling, and a lot of the destructive behavior has come from the intense self-focus of people on all sides of the conversation. As we have begun to recognize and repent of some of that intensely self-centered behavior, we are finding our spirits renewed for loving others, including those with whom we've been most enmeshed in our own communities. Finding positive regard for those with whom we've differed has unleashed the ability to love others whom we've ignored in this recent season.

While some of the practical details remain to be worked out—for example, the bishop of the Diocese of Pittsburgh, the Right Reverend Dorsey McConnell, announced in the fall of 2013 that his inclination was to allow individual churches to enter periods of listening and discernment to determine if they in good conscience could bless homosexual unions—the denomination has moved inexorably in the direction of love and acceptance for all.

It's not the first time the Church has been ahead of society—and ahead of some of its members, precipitating crisis—on an issue where society ultimately arrived in the place that the Church landed. Nor is it the first time that the Episcopal Church has lost members who felt, in good conscience, that they could not follow the Church where it was going—even though the Church turned out to be on the right side of history,.

These conflicts that have marked the last fifty years of the Episcopal Church—the years of so-called decline, and certainly the losses in numbers and prestige—have largely been conflicts about justice and inclusion. While from our vantage point today we might ask how some of these issues needed to be debated, each was a turning point at which the Church was at one point sharply divided. One of the gifts of the Anglican tradition, remember, is that people holding opposing opinions can meet under the umbrella of common worship and all call themselves Episcopalian.

So it was that in 1963, two white Episcopal bishops in Alabama were among the religious leaders who signed an open letter decrying the actions of the "outsider" Martin Luther King in Birmingham; Dr. King's "Letter from a Birmingham Jail" was written in response to their "Call for Unity." Two years later, in Alabama, the white Episcopal seminarian

Jonathan Daniels stepped in front of a shotgun blast meant for an African American civil rights worker and was killed. In that same year, John Hines was elected presiding bishop of the Episcopal Church, and he took the Church on a controversial journey in which he led the fight against racism, economic inequality, and the exclusion of blacks and women from Church ministry. Many churches withheld their support of the national church during these years, but Bishop Hines is said to have remarked that trying to continue with business as usual at such a time was like rearranging the deck chairs on the Titanic; it was meaningless action that denied the reality of the trauma unfolding all around.

Bishop Hines's call for justice began at home, but it did not end here. In 1971, at a shareholder's meeting for General Motors, he supported divestment in South Africa, one of the earliest protests against that nation's policy of apartheid racial separation. This divestment movement spread to other large corporations, who were encouraged to cut or even end their investments in that racially divided nation. Archbishop Desmond Tutu later recalled that the movement was an important part of the eventual triumph over apartheid.

When people look back on Bishop Hines's tenure in office now, they see that even if some of the programs they tried to launch had questionable efficacy, he and the Episcopal Church were on the right side of the battle against racism and for justice and economic equality. At the same time, it's impossible not to notice that being right had real costs to the Church, financial and personal alike. Some Episcopalians preferred to think of their church membership in terms of their settled Sunday worship, their social networks, and their position in the community. They might have been happy to do good things for their near neighbors, to give to charity, but these radical calls to turn the entire Episcopal Church upside down were more than they could bear, and they withheld their money—or even themselves—as a result.

Real change always comes with real cost.

The same could be said of the fight over women's ordination. It was a long and tangled trail, marked again by disagreement. When a group of women candidates ("The Philadelphia Eleven") were ordained to the priesthood by sympathetic bishops in 1974, their attempts to exercise their priestly functions caused a stir. Fellow priests who invited them

to celebrate the Eucharist were punished, while an emergency meeting of the House of Bishops denounced the ordinations and ruled that
they were invalid. After two years of turmoil, the General Convention
at last approved the ordination of women in 1976, but it remained (and
in some place, remains) controversial, another issue over which some
Episcopalians were willing to leave the Church if it happened (and others, if it didn't happen!). Three dioceses in the Episcopal Church refused
to recognize the authority of women priests well into the twenty-first
century, although the first woman bishop, Barbara Harris, was elected
in 1988, and Katharine Jefferts Schori was elected presiding bishop of
the Episcopal Church in 2006. (This, by the way, set off a firestorm of
controversy, considering that many of our Anglican brothers and sisters
do not yet believe that woman should be ordained to all the offices of the
Church; the Church of England itself just agreed to the election of women
bishops in its July 2014 Synod).

   In each of these battles of the Episcopal Culture Wars, biblical authority and the Church's history have been balanced against shifts in the culture and in our understanding of God's call to us, and the most inclusive,
just, and loving choices have been affirmed. Although these tumultuous
times have caused many hard feelings—and thinned the ranks of people
calling themselves Episcopalian—they have also brought new people into
our churches.

   I am one of them. I chose to formally align myself with the Episcopal
Church in 2003 because of their inclusive stance on GLBT persons. I
know and love many people who are gay Christians, people who have
been shunned by families, friends, and churches because of who they are.
Like many people, I thought that biblically-based prejudice against gays
was the totality of the Christianity response. Then I encountered the radical hospitality of St. James' Episcopal, Austin, a church whose African
American founders had decided that all people who entered their doors
would be welcomed, no matter what their gender, color, sexual orientation, or political party! It was an amazing vision of love and acceptance
for this recovering evangelical who grew up being told that God couldn't
possibly accept some people because of who and how they were. While,
like the Episcopal Church, I had to make a journey from my old supposi-
tions, I had gradually come to see that the old condemnations just didn't

fit with my experience of the faithful gay Christians I had known and loved—and how could the God of Love possibly be less loving than I was?

Perhaps it's no wonder that the Culture Wars have come in recent years, when other shifts have been taking place in the religious landscape. All three of these issues—racial prejudice, gender equality, and human sexuality—emerge from understandings of the Bible and how God wants us to live together. Phyllis Tickle has often spoken of how every five hundred years the Church holds a garage sale and gets rid of the things that no longer fit, and how we are in the midst of just such a transformation right now. From the late Renaissance Protestant position in which scripture is privileged as the primary authority describing how we are to live—if some verse in scripture says that the races and genders are unequal or that gays are to be condemned, who are we to disagree? — we are moving into a contemporary reality in which we understand God's authority to be revealed in different ways.

Whether we talk about the growth of something called "Emerging Christianity," or simply think of what we have now as the ultimate product of decades of discussion and evolution, there is little question that the Episcopal Church is a different creature today than it was in 1960. It is also different in many ways from other Christian denominations in 2015 still wrestling with the culture wars in their own traditions (or unwilling even to start wrestling because they still live within scriptural paradigms that they don't want to question).

That difference may be one of the primary reasons we can reach out to a culture full of people who feel alone, marginalized, afraid, or put off by conflict, hatred, or hypocrisy. Despite all the hardship, the hard feelings, the losses, and the tears, we have come to the other side of the culture wars and wound up in a place that makes sense according to a theology of a loving and welcoming God—and the theology that the Church, who stands in for God, must also be loving and welcoming. Happily, this decision also puts us in a place of cultural relevance. While many Americans look at Christianity with suspicion and even disdain because of its targeted stance against homosexuality and women, the Episcopal Church has the chance to show that one can love God and love and serve all your neighbors, regardless of who they are or whom they love.

I'd like to close this section with words from my friend Bob Kinney, for many years the communications director at the Episcopal Seminary of the Southwest. Bob is not an Episcopalian, exactly, although his job as communications director means that he did directly witness many changes in the Church, many shifts in the education of priests and other church leaders, and many worship services.

I'm sure he thought he'd seen everything.

But when St. David's, Austin, blessed the union of parishioners Anthony Chapple and Dennis Driskell, the first same-sex blessing in the Diocese of Texas (Anthony and Dennis married in New York, but Texas does not, as of this writing, recognize gay marriage), Bob was the photographer for that blessed event, and it sparked many reflections for him about the past, our history together at the Seminary of the Southwest, and the future of the Episcopal Church:

> You won't find any cross inside Christ Chapel on the campus of the Episcopal Seminary of the Southwest in Austin where Dr. Greg Garrett is writer-in-residence and I was communications director for twenty-four years. Instead, purposely, the cross stands outside the chapel and provides a symbolic background to the altar inside.
>
> The iconic twenty-second presiding bishop John Hines—who founded the seminary when he was bishop of the Diocese of Texas in the 1950s—wanted to emphasize that "the Church exists for those outside its walls." Hines became presiding bishop in 1965 when the Civil Rights Era and other needed societal changes were transforming our country, and John vigorously led the Church into the Waters of Justice.
>
> Anthony and Dennis's historic blessing in Texas no doubt made John Hines smile. I bet the legendary preacher wished he could have preached at their service.
>
> I ended my article about this heartfelt service by writing, "It was the most stunningly spiritual experience I have had in a church throughout my [then] sixty-six years."[20]
>
> Too often all faiths sadly settle for worship that is stale and lifeless because "we have always done it that way." This numbing predictability is passed on from generation to generation until someone

finally asks "Why aren't people—especially young adults—coming to our church?"

The heartfelt cosmic joy throughout the St. David's sanctuary flowing from family, parishioners and other friends during the blessing is what Real Church should feel like every time we gather together. This goal is reachable if we really love each other as we love ourselves both in and outside the church walls.

It was fun to see partners Sarah Kapostasy and Mel Zidkowski with their newborn daughter Hadley in a St. David's pew. This segues nicely into a more recent joyful church experience I had at St. Mary Magdalene Church in Manor, just outside Austin.

SMM is a diverse, vibrant, multigenerational, and growing congregation of about ninety folks who hold their Sunday service in the Manor High School cafeteria until they will move into an innovative Diocese of Texas "moveable church" at Christmastide. A huge video screen presenting both the Spanish and English words of hymns hovers above the altar while a young adult four-piece band plays lively church music throughout the one-hour service.

"Many folks come to SMM seeking something different," said the Reverend Alex Montes-Vela. "Some were unchurched before joining us, while others had unhappy experiences in their former church.

"Several families with young children felt their previous church simply tolerated their toddlers. SMM welcomes all, from babies to eighty-year-olds, and all participate in our Mass," he said.

I especially like one of the many photos I shot of the service. Taken from the back, it shows a standing little girl dressed in white hugging two men who were seated in front of her. I e-mailed Reverend Montes-Vela for the names of the girl and her father and maybe uncle. "Those are her two dads," he wrote back to me. I was honored to have that photo posted on the SMM Facebook page on Father's Day.

Someday, please God, all such answers will be as matter-of-fact as the one the Reverend Alex Montes-Vela gave to Bob Kinney. But for now, in a nation that remains deeply divided about the place of gays and lesbians in society and in the church, I give thanks that my Church has come down firmly on the side of love. It is this sort of radical and inclusive love that makes change possible in those who seek to do it and in those who witness it. It explains the peak spiritual experience Bob received at the same-sex blessing—and it underlies one of my favorite stories about transformation, about the time my mom came to visit St. James' Episcopal with its rich tapestry of races and sexual preferences.

I had, I confess, some worries about her coming to church with me. My mother has traveled the world, but she grew up in a small town in Oklahoma where racism was unconscious, and the Baptist churches in which she'd spent most of her adult life were not the most tolerant when it came to gays and lesbians, so I wondered how she would react to worship that was full of African American spirituals, mixed-race couples, and same-gender couples.

As the service went on, I kept sneaking sideways glances, but I couldn't read anything. Her joy—or her contempt—were veiled. But then as people began to file down the center aisle to take the Eucharist, I could feel her start to shake next to me.

"Here we go," I thought. A mixed-race lesbian couple were leading their daughter down to partake of the bread and wine, and I assumed that this had pushed my mom over the edge. She was shaking with rage, I thought, filled with disgust, probably one moment from rising and fleeing the church.

Then I heard the noise, and realized the truth.

My mother, my seventy-year-old mother from Red-State Oklahoma, was not shaking with anger. She was weeping. Tears were sliding down her face as she watched the rainbow people of St. James' lined up to receive communion, and she just looked over at me and shook her head.

"It's so beautiful," she whispered. "This must be what heaven looks like."

Yes, I nodded back, my own tears in my eyes. It must be. Heaven must be this gathering of all God's children—including the ones who didn't realize they belonged in a gathering of all God's children.

I have never again discounted how radical love and inclusion can change the world. My hope—my prayer—for the Episcopal Church is that all of us will make this love and acceptance widely known, that we will stand up for love and justice not only in our pews but in the outside world, where everyone can see it and have the chance to be changed by it.

Questions for Discussion

1. What is your conception of the Bible and its authority? If you find something troubling in the Bible, how would you address it? (Remember our conversation in Chapter Four about doing Anglican theology!)
2. Why do you think churches have sought to exclude people instead of include them? What sort of theology would argue for this?
3. What arguments have you heard (or perhaps even used yourself) for or against the ordination of women to places of church leadership? What response would you make to those who argue that the Bible seems to limit women to smaller roles than men?
4. President Barack Obama (who sometimes attends St. John's Episcopal Church in Washington, DC) recently supported gay marriage after what he described as a slow shifting on the issue. Have your own views undergone any evolution on the place of gays in the Church and in society? If yes, what has helped to changed them?

For Further Reading

Eugene Robinson, *God Believes in Love: Straight Talk about Gay Marriage* (New York: Vintage, 2013).

Bishop Robinson addresses ten questions skeptics often have about whether gay marriage is moral or biblical, and he does so gently, drawing on not only his personal experience as a gay man seeking to marry, but also his deep study of and reverence for scripture and the Church's teachings.

Katharine Jefferts Schori, *The Heartbeat of God: Finding the Sacred in the Middle of Everything* (Woodstock, VT: Skylight Paths Publications, 2010).

In this book by the first female primate (head of a national church) in the history of the Anglican tradition, Bishop Jefferts Schori argues for wide inclusion of women and those on the margins, and for the connectedness of everyone and everything.

Desmond Tutu, *The Rainbow People of God: The Making of a Peaceful Revolution* (New York: Random House, 1996).

This collection of Bishop Tutu's visionary speeches during the struggle against apartheid in South Africa is also a vision of inclusion and acceptance. The metaphor he chooses for his title represents the Church at its very best!

Telling the World: Evangelism for a World That Hates Evangelism but Needs the Church

I grew up in the American South and in Oklahoma, two regions of the United States where Christianity is still a part of the cultural ethos. When people meet, it is not rare that one will ask the other, "What church do you go to?" And if the other doesn't go to church, or doesn't have a current church home, it wouldn't be at all unusual for the asker to proffer an invitation to church, or even to ask the underlying question: "Are you a Christian?" (I still get that last one, by the way—including that version of it from my grandmother who wondered if Episcopalians believe in Jesus!)

When I received my first sabbatical from Baylor University, my former wife and I went out to the Pacific Northwest. She had been an evangelical Christian when I first met her, and had been shedding bits and pieces of that identity. Me? I didn't much like to be around Christians because where we lived they were constantly asking questions like "What church do you go to?" and "Are you a Christian?" So, we came to an agreement that we should look for a church while we were in Oregon. Only, we couldn't find anybody who could make a recommendation to us.

That is, we didn't meet any Christians who invited us to be part of their communities. No one I knew through the University of Oregon, where I was teaching that semester, attended church. None of my students did, either. No one we met in our neighborhood, or in the stores where we shopped, or in the bakery where I bought way too many cream cheese brownies seemed interested in talking about church.

Now, a few pagans were willing to talk with us, gently, about their communities, and we did see plenty of their bumper stickers on cars around town:

"Blessed be."

"My other car is a broomstick."

"Back off, I'm a goddess!"

But no one seemed willing to claim Christianity. And while we finally visited a couple of churches (Baptist and Presbyterian) in that church-spare area, the members seemed almost unwilling to greet us. It wasn't until the third church that anyone actually even said hello to us, and that's why, for several months, we became Presbyterian.

Now I know I am speaking of two very different realities (Christian South, meet Post-Christian Northwest). But I also know that, all theologies aside, on the whole, I liked the pagans a lot more than I liked the Christians. They were nicer. They weren't so pushy—or, in the case of the Oregonian Christians, so frosty. They left room for me to believe what I wanted to believe.

Since becoming one of them, I've discovered that Episcopalians tend to be more like the pagans in this regard (and, skeptics might remark, in others!). They don't push their beliefs down people's throats, they often wait for people to ask before they speak up, and they often tell people what they believe largely by putting bumper stickers on their car:

"God loves you. No exceptions."

"Love God. Love Your Neighbor. Change the World."

"The Episcopal Church Welcomes Everyone!"

Those are nice sentiments, and those moving billboards do sometimes catch the eye of people who need to see them. The spirit moves, and our cars are in the right place at the right time. Katie Sherrod, a layperson from Fort Worth whose husband is the Reverend Gayland Pool, tells a story about a time when bumper-sticker evangelism led to a great outcome. Like many of us, she has a bumper sticker talking about how the Episcopal Church welcomes all (two stickers, actually, one in English and one in Spanish), and she blogged the story about a young man who saw her bumper sticker, pulled up beside her at a traffic light, and asked her to roll down her window:

> What follows is my best memory of an encounter that lasted only a minute or less. The young man said, "Thank you! Thank you!"
>
> I obviously looked puzzled and he said, "Thank you for your support of same sex marriage. Your church is awesome. The Episcopal Church is awesome."
>
> "I said, 'Yes, it is,'" and smiled at him.
>
> "We are getting married in July (not in Texas)," he said. I offered two thumbs up. "Thank your church," he said.
>
> Then the light changed and he turned right. I started forward to merge onto I-30, smiling and lost in gratitude for the decades-long work of so many faithful LGBT Episcopalians and allies who are loving my church into becoming a transforming force in so many lives, both in the wider church, and now, at last, here in my diocese.
>
> I am proud to be an Episcopalian.[21]

I too am proud to be an Episcopalian, as I trust this book evidences. More than proud. My identity as an Episcopal follower of Christ is one of the central defining elements of who I am.

I have found joy and life and community in the Episcopal Church.

I discovered my vocation in the Episcopal Church.

I encountered most of my best friends through the Episcopal Church.

I met my wife in the Episcopal Church.

And in addition to all those great and good things, I know that without one particular Episcopal church, one particular Episcopal priest, and the great and good gifts of the tradition as a whole, I would not be around today to talk about all the things I love about the Episcopal Church.

I owe so much to the Church that, at times, I am baffled why everyone else doesn't see all the wonders I see.

And then I am forced to ask: Why should they see all those wonders when they aren't being brought to their attention? I mean, I do have a sticker on my car. Bumper sticker evangelism is one way to try to broadcast the good news we have discovered in our tradition. But if the continued decline in membership in the national church and in many local churches means anything—and Lucinda Laird, dean of the American Cathedral in Paris, convinced me that while numbers should not be our sole worry, they do measure some things that matter—it probably means that Episcopalians need to find some additional and perhaps some better ways to tell others about the Church, about our own particular congregations, about our faith, and about how God is moving in the world. And, of course, we need to do it in such a way that we don't remind people of pushy Christians, since that tends to reinforce all the negative impressions they have about all of us.

Kirk Royal writes from North Carolina, "I'm in the 'let's reclaim the word *evangelism*' camp. . . . I think one way we're doing it is by meeting people where they are instead of shouting that we expect them to come to us, and on our 'terms.' Now that we're doing that, I'm just wondering when we'll finally get up the nerve as a body to call it exactly what it is: evangelism. It's not a dirty word, folks."

The problem is that evangelism is a four-letter word for many Episcopalians and, now, for much of secular society as well. We are uncomfortable with the models we've witnessed, and for much of our history, we haven't had to think about evangelizing. Traditionally, drawing people to the Episcopal tradition looked like this: If people wanted to experience beautiful worship—or hobnob with city leaders and bank presidents—they would eventually find their way in the doors of our churches.

If we build St. Swithin's—"St Swithin's," it may someday behoove you to know, is Anglican/Episcopal slang for any hypothetical church, anywhere; sometimes we refer to our Everychurch as "St. Swithin's in the Swamp"—if we build St. Swithin's, they will come.

Only the world doesn't operate that way anymore. We have lots of St. Swithin'ses scattered across this land. They are beautiful churches. People want to get married in them; we turn couples away. But do they want to become and remain part of our communities after they get married in our sanctuaries or in our rose gardens? Generally, sadly, no.

Church attendance in the US, while still stronger than many other places in the Western world, is not an automatic assumption anymore. The Nones, as we have noted, are now the fastest-growing group in religious surveys, and membership in the Episcopal Church (as with other mainline Protestant denominations) is not the executive club it once seemed to be. As the Reverend Dr. Samuel Lloyd, rector of Trinity Boston (and former dean of the National Cathedral) puts it, the main challenges to the Episcopal Church these days come from two facts: We are unaccustomed to being outside the established mainstream, and we don't know who we are (yet) if we aren't at the very center of things.[22]

Many of us don't know yet, that is, how to do something besides open the doors—or open the doors and put a sign up outside—or open the doors, put a sign up, and run an ad in the newspaper (if such things even exist anymore). That suggests that there are a couple of things that we need to think about if we are going to tell people about the tradition we're from, the good work being done by the particular church we love, and the amazing people working alongside us for the Kingdom of God.

The first of those things: We need to engage with others, in lots of ways, about what God is doing in our lives and in the life of the Church.

There's a lovely old nineteenth-century hymn, sung often by Quakers, offered up most memorably in the last hundred years, perhaps, by Pete Seeger and Enya. It's called "How Can I Keep From Singing?" and you probably know it. My favorite verse goes:

> No storm can shake my inmost calm
> While to that refuge clinging;
> Since Christ is Lord of Heav'n and earth,
> How can I keep from singing?

That question is not rhetorical. If Christ is Lord of Heaven and earth— if God is moving in the world, and in my life—how can I be silent about it? And yet, too often, I fear we *are* silent about it, hoping that our priests or the sign over the door or something else will speak up for us.

We don't have to walk up to strangers on the street, ask if they are Christian, and invite them to church, although inviting people to church would be a huge step forward for many of us. Telling people that they are welcome somewhere, anywhere, is one of the best bits of good news I know, especially when many people don't feel welcome in their homes or in their own bodies. The Reverend David Boyd, rector of St. David's, Austin, returned from a sabbatical spent traveling in the UK to remark on his favorite British phrase: "You are very welcome." How lovely, he preached, for anyone to say to us, "You are very welcome here." How necessary, in fact, that we let everyone we encounter know that our church is a place where they are—and will feel—very welcome.

Passing on some wisdom or letting them know you care might also be ways of making people feel welcome. The Reverend Mary Certain Vano from Little Rock says that a project that her congregation is continuing is the use of "quotation cards": "I invite people to give me their favorite quotes from scripture or other popular bits of wisdom. Then we print them on business cards (with church info on the back). It's an encouraging and less intimidating way to share grace, along with an invitation to come and see."

Bishop Andy Doyle has similar advice: We need to be ready to hand out information about our churches in a way that seems welcoming and authentic.

> We need to be ready to talk about our church and not stumble around looking for something to say . . . "uhhhhhhhhh." This is not an acceptable answer for why we love our church. I know a church that is trying to get it down to three things. What are the three things you like about your church? Go. Name three things. Write them down. Memorize them. Make sure they are the best three things you can think of. Then, pick up some business cards from the church office. (Or maybe your church has some MOO cards [creative business cards] to hand out; these have the address and website info for the church *and* service times). Now you are ready to go.

Some of us (whether because we are introverts, because we are Episcopalians, or because we are both) would still find that kind of encounter difficult. Thankfully, we can offer our involvement and thoughtful engagement as evangelism as well. Sometimes what people respond to best are listening and care. The Right Reverend Greg Rickel is somewhat famous for barroom evangelism; he has told me (and others) about his ongoing friendship with a Seattle bartender. After some time, the bartender asked him what he did, and was surprised to discover that Greg was a bishop. (He seemed like such a nice guy!) The Reverend Bill Fulton, who serves in Silverdale, Washington, recalls Greg telling the story about the bartender to clergy from the Diocese of Olympia:

So when Christmas came near, [the bartender] asked Greg where he was going to be for Christmas. Greg said, "The cathedral. Would you like to come?"

The bartender said, "Where do I sit?"

Greg commented to us, "That's a very interesting question. He was worried about crossing the boundary into the church and where he would sit. We should remember that when we think about newcomers." So Greg arranged that someone would meet the bartender at the door of the cathedral so he could sit with Greg's family.

At Easter, the same thing happened and the bartender brought some friends to the cathedral where Greg was. Now he's exploring other Episcopal churches.

For many of us, evangelism is about engagement and relationship, not just about sharing information. As Greg's bartender story points out, people who might be put off by our initiating contact could also be deeply spiritual people who need some of the things we can offer. The Reverend Erin Warde also speaks of the importance of relational evangelism:

I think the biggest tool that I have for evangelism is listening. Also growing up evangelical, that often seemed like it was the missing piece to the evangelism I was experiencing and offering. We didn't listen to people, and no one listened to me. Now, I try to listen, empathize, pray for, and encourage. Those are things I believe Christ did when he encountered people, and I would hope that those things can offer Christ-like healing.

Finally, the Reverend Pam Graham, who serves in Rockdale, Texas, told me a story that nicely illustrates the various kinds of evangelism about which we're talking:

I was at a meeting with administrators and superintendent of the schools here in town with the ministerial alliance (small town). The purpose of the meeting was to brainstorm how we could all band together to help the children of the community. One "true to the known use of evangelical" preacher said, "Well if I can't use the words Jesus Christ and tell how He is our Lord and Savior, how can I witness?" I mentioned that by our very being with the children, they would know Jesus because he lives in us and speaks and acts through

us. He gave me a very dirty look, but the super thanked me afterward.
So, Greg, I just be me to evangelize, and invite when asked.

Like Pam, I try to live with kindness, and to manifest the God who
has healed and changed me, and people do sometimes ask me about my life
because there is something in it that appeals to them. I much prefer this
sort of evangelizing to the sort on which I was raised—the pointed evangelism of the pastor in Pam's story. I know I'm not alone in that. Many of
us happily misquote St. Francis, who is supposed to have said, "Preach at
all times. Use words when necessary." (He didn't, although his Rule does
say "Let all the brothers, however, preach by their deeds.")[23] Still, the idea
behind this quotation is a powerful one, as these stories remind us.

For those of us who struggle with the verbal invitation, it's nice to
know that being a welcoming presence can take many forms: a church
coffee shop where people get a hot cup of something and a smile on their
way to work, a food ministry where we feed people good hot meals for a
reasonable price, a farmers' market where people can buy fresh produce.

And welcoming people into our churches for any reason—for food,
coffee, ESL classes, and 12-step programs, the cancer support group we
find meeting in an Episcopal Church in the novel *The Fault in Our Stars*,
for concerts and fundraisers, even for a meeting of the Rotary Club—all
offer us a chance to show others outside the tradition that we are more
than a building that opens up for worship on Sunday morning. It can
allow them to see our values at work. It can be a way of preaching without speaking.

But we have to do more than that. Sometimes we need to speak! (I
do recognize the irony of my being a licensed lay preacher who finds it
hard—outside the narrow confines of the pulpit—to tell the good news.)
Bishop Doyle's suggestion that we need a clear and succinct message about
the blessings we've encountered in the tradition for a world so full of data
and distraction leads me to my second conclusion. We have to push out
the message about our churches and our faith in a multitude of ways, and
many churches and individuals in the Episcopal Church do just that.

It's not enough for me to have a bumper sticker on my car, not enough
for me to tell individuals I meet that I'm part of a wonderful church body
and tradition. It's not enough to hope that people will magically come in

the door of my church and be moved by beauty and music and my most excellent sermon. I happen to be married to a church communicator, and as my wife, Jeanie, knows better than most folks, telling people about the Church is a full-time job.

These days, Jeanie's work on behalf of the Church is, she says, about juggling the old and the new ways of telling. Some people still read church bulletins, or respond to other kinds of print, but even more important, she says, are the new ways that people communicate now. E-mail and social media are a vital part of getting our message out in the twenty-first century, and not just to members. They're also a way of speaking to people who don't yet (and may never) have a formal association with our churches. Jeanie said that the hospitality ministry at St. David's, Austin, has its own Facebook page and its own distinct audience. "Our Café Divine Facebook [page] is aimed at downtown workers who visit the church for Thursday lunch. They have a special bond with Chef Ray, and love seeing what he's up to that day! For many of them, this is the only reason they come into St. David's (same for Holy Grounds [the St. David's coffee shop])."

Meredith Gould, a layperson from Baltimore who happens to be married to the Reverend Dan Webster, is a former church communications director who has written fine books on communication and on social media (I recommend the recent *Social Media Gospel* in this book). She told me her story of coming to understand the importance of all sorts of communication:

> Eventually I was hired to manage communications for a large suburban parish. We were still producing and mailing quarterly newsletters; the website was being held hostage by the only person who could code HTML. I also served for two years as a communications consultant at the diocesan level where, again, almost everything was printed and mailed and probably tossed right into recycling bins.
>
> That experience inspired me to write *The Word Made Fresh: Communicating Church and Faith Today* (Morehouse) because I could see that communications was an essential ministry of the church but not being treated with the same level of reverence as, say, the music or youth ministries.

When it comes to social media, I'm fond of pointing out that I was involved with social media before it was even called social media—during the early 1990s, when chat rooms and bulletin boards provided an online gathering place for like-minded and -hearted people.

I'd have to say—and I don't think this is euphoric recall—that I almost instantly recognized how twenty-first century social media platforms could and would make a difference by allowing people to move beyond doing church to being church for one another beyond the narrow confines of time, space, place, and denomination.

I view social media as the most dramatic and perhaps radical tool for communication that we've seen in a very long time. These tools allow people to connect without having their faith mediated (or controlled) by the institutional church and its structures of authority.

A pertinent sidenote: On the day I was drafting this chapter, Meredith tweeted the following: "Remember that social media makes it possible to reach and inspire many more people than we can f2f." As we'll also see in our chapter on being the church all week long, social media can be a vital part of a twenty-first century Church that touches, supports, and prays for each other and the world every day of the week—and when we are on social media, our message is out there for many people to see.

In some ways, I will grant you, it is a new version of bumper sticker evangelism, but it also allows us to be ourselves, as Erin Warde and other respondents advocate. When people see me tweeting about my church, my next sermon, or about my faith (particularly when they've followed me because they love my writing, or because something funny or inspirational I said that one time inspired their interest), I'm not Pastor Greg, coming toward them with a predatory smile and an agenda. I'm just Greg—or at worst, Dr. Garrett—that writer who likes *Guardians of the Galaxy* and U2 and great restaurants and who happens to be a passionate follower of Christ through the Episcopal tradition.

The same goes for Facebook. It can be a tool for engaging people in the process of being authentic about my faith, beliefs, doubts, and fears. On the morning that I drafted this chapter in Wales, I posted this message on the tail end of a week that saw war in Gaza and bombing in Iraq, the suicide of Robin Williams, and the death of Lauren Bacall, one piece of hard news after another: "Today in the calendar of the Church we remember the life of Florence Nightingale, the founder of modern nursing, and all those who seek to bring healing to the afflicted, comfort to the broken, presence to the dying, and hope to the hopeless. May we be of their number, with God's help. Amen."

Below that I posted a clarifying comment: "Feeling especially worn down by this week of war and loss and suicide. And yet, we are all God has, this raggedy helping army as Annie Lamott calls us. Love hard today!"

As a somewhat successful writer and semiprivate figure, I have many more friends and followers on Facebook than I actually have friends in real life. My Facebook friends (like yours, I'm guessing) come from all over the world and from all walks of life, and while hundreds of mine are indeed Episcopalian (isn't it a rule that you have to be Facebook friends with every other member of the Episcopal Church?), many of them are blissfully agnostic or cheerfully unchurched. But all of them are spiritual beings, all of them have some sort of hole in their hearts, and while they might never set foot in one of our churches, they nonetheless need spiritual care as much as any of us.

Meredith Gould noted how social media allowed us to touch people outside the walls of the Church—one of the topics of our two remaining chapters. But the other, our chapter on doing justice, is linked to evangelism because it is also work we do outside the walls of the Church (and I happen to know about many instances of Episcopalians doing justice work because of Facebook, interestingly enough). Many of my Episcopal sisters and brothers have been involved in protests, in rallies, and in very public demonstrations of faith in action. I think particularly of gay pride parades, where I have seen pictures of parishioners (gay and straight alike) marching in solidarity and love, of priests and bishops in clerical collars or even full clerical gear marching as representatives of a tradition that doesn't believe anyone is excluded from the love of God.

What Christians do in the public eye—for good or ill—is evangelism, because it tells people who we are. If we want people to walk alongside us, in marches or in the larger world, we need to be a people of love, justice, compassion, and mercy. I'd like to be a part of that club.

Just tell me when the meetings are—

And offer to sit with me, so I won't feel out of place.

Questions for Discussion

1. When you hear the word "evangelism," what thoughts or images come to mind? Have you been the victim of evangelism done wrong (or the lucky recipient of evangelism done right)?
2. "Evangelism" comes from the words "good news," and is ultimately about communicating good news to the world. If you had to boil down that good news about your church or your faith to three things, what would they be?
3. If you are part of a faith community, what things is your community doing to let people outside your church know who and what you are? How successful do you think these efforts have been?
4. If you were called to be an evangelist (and, apparently, all Episcopalians are called to service and evangelism), what would your preferred method of evangelism be?

For Further Reading

Diana Butler Bass, *Christianity for the Rest of Us: How the Neighborhood Church Is Transforming the Faith* (New York: HarperOne, 2007).

Bass, a historian and Episcopal layperson, brings together a book on the successful practices of a number of mainstream churches who are in growth rather than decline. Here are things you might brag about, if you see them happening in your churches—or things you might be *doing* in your churches!

Yvonne Richmond, Stephen Croft, et al., *Evangelism in a Spiritual Age: Communicating Faith in a Changing Culture* (London: Church House, 2005).

All of us are entering a world where the traditional ways of inviting people to become church members are changing, and our culture militates against membership in *anything*. This collection of contemporary essays from the Church of England explores the even more challenging problem of evangelism in the UK, but the ideas are easily transferable to Episcopal churches.

Eric Law, *Inclusion: Making Room for Grace* (St. Louis: Chalice, 2000).

The Reverend Law is an expert on multiculturalism, inclusion, and church growth, and in this book he writes about the importance of reaching out to bring others into your church—and about some of the personal and structural barriers that might make that hard to do.

Doing Justice:
A Church That Works

I n the fall of my second year in seminary, I was given my field placement. That meant that for the next two years I was going to be attached as a sort of priest-in-training to a new church where I'd been matched through a process something like being sorted for a house at Hogwarts, and there I would learn the behind-the-scenes details about faith, practice, and church management that watching Greg Rickel preach and preside on Sunday had not yet given me. My assignment was Calvary Episcopal in Bastrop, Texas, a lovely and historic little church about forty minutes outside of Austin.

From everything I'd heard from others and during the process of my assignment, I had the impression that my placement at Calvary was going to serve two purposes. I was going to learn from my rector, the Reverend Matt Zimmerman, about what a priest does and how he does it, and I was expecting to observe this new community to see how a church operates. For my part, I was guessing that I would give something back to that community by teaching and preaching, two things I did pretty well and would learn to do even better. But just after I arrived in August 2005, something happened that made it clear that I would be learning much more from them than they would ever learn from me.

That something was Hurricane Katrina. It smashed a path across the Gulf Coast from Florida to Texas, killing almost two thousand people (over a hundred people are still categorized as "missing"), wiping homes, businesses, schools, and churches off the map, or flooding them, as it did in New Orleans.

I was in shock. As a longtime lover of New Orleans, I had long talked with dear friends there about how someday the city would get hit by "the Big One," but somehow we never believed it would happen. Like everyone, I was heartbroken by the news and images coming out of the city.

I was in shock, but the good people of Calvary Episcopal were not. The first Sunday after the hurricane, they were already organizing. People were gathering things to send to the Gulf region, and others were already planning to go and help the residents to rebuild. It was clear that not only were we at Calvary going to pray for those afflicted by this terrible natural disaster, but we were going to do tangible hands-on things to try to make their lives better. People were going to set aside their own lives to help those in need. They were going to live out their faith in a tangible way that I wasn't sure I had ever witnessed before, because, frankly, I hadn't lived it out much myself.

Fay Jones and her husband, Pete, led Calvary's response to Katrina, and ended up staying and working on the Mississippi Gulf Coast for six months, from the immediate response to the disaster through the snarled recovery period and into the time when people began to recover and rebuild. Fay recently shared a few of her memories of and reflections on that powerful time with me, saying that where Katrina had brought devastation, Episcopalians and hippies brought healing!

In September 2005, my husband, Pete Jones, was invited to join a group of Christian men from Bastrop County, Texas, on a mission to the people of Waveland, Mississippi, which had been devastated by Hurricane Katrina. After a week in the very primitive camp on a parking lot in Waveland, Pete was asked to be the operations manager of the mission because he was retired and the other men needed to return home to work and families. At that time, I joined Pete in Waveland. A family in Bastrop had donated the use of a travel trailer, and this became our home until after Christmas that year.

Soon after the storm, the Rainbow People, a group of hippies, set up camp in conjunction with our camp. They set up a massive kitchen and prepared three nutritious meals a day for the volunteers and for the now homeless residents of the Mississippi Gulf Coast.

At the height of our time in Waveland, we were feeding and serving approximately 1,500 people a day. Although the market and the
kitchen were intended to serve the people of Waveland, no one was
turned away in the beginning.

While many of our volunteers worked in the market, many also
worked out in the community clearing out houses, removing debris,
and other activities. Our volunteers came from all walks of life, and
many denominations—Methodist, Lutheran, Presbyterian, and
Episcopal. I can't say enough about our volunteers. They arrived at
all times of day or night and were anxious to go right to work. We
started them off with a tour of the city so they could experience
the extent of the devastation. We explained that while they were
welcome to encourage the survivors to tell their story, no one was to
press for information. We never entered the "space" of a residence
unless invited by the homeowner.

Where was God in all this? God was in the tremendous outpouring of compassion across this country, which resulted in money,
clothing, and food being sent immediately to those who had lost
everything. God was in the faces, hands, and hearts of the hundreds of volunteers who came to Mississippi to assist in rebuilding
peoples' homes and lives. God was in the prayers we offered every
morning and evening, asking for wisdom, patience, and some measure of understanding of the experience.

Our sending church was Calvary Episcopal Church in Bastrop,
Texas. Father Matt Zimmermann led a group to Waveland. We had
the support of prayer and other donations. One Sunday when Pete
and I had returned home for some much-needed R & R, Father Matt
asked me to speak on our experience from the pulpit.

What did I take away from Katrina? Humility, a renewed sense
of compassion, hope in humanity, faith that God is with us and in
us and using us to reconcile and heal. Just as we witnessed the best
in people, we also witnessed greed, anger, hopelessness. But this
did not dampen our spirits or cause us to stop doing our best. My
faith is stronger, and I believe I have more patience and am more
willing to "not sweat the little things" than before spending six
months where Katrina had truly leveled the playing field and made
all equal.

Humility, a renewed sense of compassion, hope in humanity, faith that God is with us and in us and using us to reconcile and heal. It's an amazingly apt definition of what Episcopalians believe about our responsibility to be about God's work of justice in the world, and the tragedy of this terrible storm offers a great opening example for us. As Fay suggests, the Episcopal Church's response to Katrina didn't just come from one small church in Bastrop, Texas. It was huge, it was nationwide, and it included many individual churches, as well as agencies of the national church.

Episcopal Relief and Development consulted with the churches and dioceses affected and began channeling resources to them. Episcopal Migration Ministries began to investigate the possibility of resettling those who had been left homeless. Most importantly, the presiding bishop, then the Right Reverend Frank Griswold, sent out a message calling on all bishops, priests, deacons, and parishioners in the Episcopal Church to respond in spiritual and tangible ways:

> I am sending this message by e-mail to our bishops, clergy and congregations—insofar as is possible—so that it might be shared and that we might be a community united in prayer and service during this time.
>
> During these past days I have been contacting bishops in the areas affected by hurricane Katrina and have spoken to the bishops of Alabama, the Central Gulf Coast, Louisiana, and Mississippi. As you would imagine, they are ministering to their communities the very best they can under extraordinarily difficult circumstances. Communication is tenuous, and in some cases impossible. As hour by hour the almost unimaginable ravages of the hurricane become more fully known we are continuing to learn of further losses of life, houses, churches, and other familiar points of reference, including the destruction of whole communities.
>
> At this time let us be exceedingly mindful that bearing one another's burdens and sharing one another's suffering is integral to being members of Christ's body. I call upon every member of our church to reach out in prayer and tangible support to our brothers and sisters as they live through these overwhelming days of loss and begin to face the difficult challenges of the future. . . .

Life affords us very few securities and yet deep within us, often revealed in the midst of profound vulnerability and loss, springs up a hope that contradicts the circumstances in which we find ourselves. Such hope emerges from the depths of despair as pure and unexpected gift. This is the way in which Christ accompanies us and seeks to share our burdens. May Christ so be with those of us who are enduring the effects of the hurricane, and may each one of us be a minister of hope to others in these dark and tragic days.

May we together pray:

God of mercy and compassion, be in our midst and bind us together in your Spirit as a community of love and service to bear one another's burdens in these days as we face the ravages of storm and sea. This we pray through Jesus Christ our Lord from whom alone comes our hope. Amen.[24]

I was stunned again, this time not by grief, but by the ways that my church, my Church, and many other church and nongovernmental organizations were present in the face of this incredible tragedy. Prayer *and* service, Bishop Griswold said. Maybe our governments were failing the test, but individuals and faith communities were rising to the task of helping their neighbors. As I looked around that small country church, as I looked at the pew where Fay and Pete Jones would normally sit, and thought about what they were all willing to do to manifest Christ's love to a despairing world, I was starting to understand what it meant to be a Christian who works for justice and peace, who stands up for those who have nothing. It looked just exactly like this.

Now why did all of these Episcopalians stand up for peace and justice? Why do any of us? Because, as you probably know, the United States is full of deeply faithful Christians who are satisfied to preach personal salvation as their primary value, and who tend to get more exercised about what they perceive as the decline in American morality than they do about the rise in Americans below the poverty line. (Let me be the first to acknowledge that many evangelical Christians, particularly younger evangelicals, would follow Jim Wallis and Brian McLaren in arguing that the Kingdom of God is about prayer and service. But so long as the cultural version of Christianity seems to many to be narrowly moral, it will need to be said and resaid that we Episcopalians are extolling a counter-cultural version of Christianity based on love and service, not on judgment and salvation.)

Why do Episcopalians love their neighbors? Sara Miles, a lay leader at St. Gregory of Nyssa in San Francisco, puts it beautifully in her book *Take This Bread*, where she details her own journey from receiving the Eucharist to starting a food bank. She describes being struck by all these strange stories of Jesus feeding people. Even after he died and returned, he was *still* feeding people. What did this mass of stories about Jesus being with people in their most basic needs have to say to her? "All of it pointed to a force stronger than the anxious formulas of religion," she concluded, "a radically inclusive love that accompanied people in the most ordinary of actions—eating, drinking, walking—and stayed with them, through fear, even past death. That love meant giving yourself away, embracing outsiders as family, emptying yourself to feed and live for others."[25]

What Sara suggests seems to be a truth of our faith. The call to love our neighbors in tangible as well as spiritual fashion is not optional. Even though some Episcopalians privilege this call more than others (Calvary was powerfully involved with service; Sara complained that her church initially resisted the idea of feeding their neighbors), this call to love God and to love our neighbor that Augustine of Hippo called the Two-Fold Commandment is enshrined in our liturgy. You can find it in our Prayers of the People, you can tease it out of various collects and sections of liturgy, and most importantly, you hear it in a section of the prayer book that many of us end up reciting several times a year, the Baptismal Covenant.

That covenant, Bishop Andy Doyle told me, was rumored to have been a late addition to the 1979 prayer book, but whenever it came along, in his estimation it represents the key to our entire Book of Common Prayer. "The Covenant," he says, "helps us find ourselves in the midst of relationship with God and with one another. It locates our spiritual journey in the midst of the spiritual journey of a whole community of faithful people. . . . It helps us discover that we come from love, move through the world in love, and are always in the process of returning to love."

When the godparents present a candidate for baptism, they recite the well-known bits you remember vaguely from *The Godfather*. They renounce Satan on behalf of their godchild. They promise, on behalf of their godchild, to follow Christ. Then the focus shifts to the congregation, who in the liturgy are actually invited to renew their faith and recommit themselves to God through repeating the Baptismal Covenant. The first parts of the covenant are about agreeing to worship together, continuously repenting of our evil, and proclaiming by word and deed the good news of God in Jesus Christ. Then we get down to the questions and affirmations that seal love of neighbor as a central belief for every Episcopalian:

> *Celebrant*   Will you seek and serve Christ in all persons, loving your neighbor as yourself?
>
> *People*   I will, with God's help.
>
> *Celebrant*   Will you strive for justice and peace among all people, and respect the dignity of every human being?
>
> *People*   I will, with God's help.

Whether or not we feel comfortable doing so, whether or not we even want to be around the poor, the dirty, the marginalized, the mentally ill, the elderly, the immigrant, and all the long list of people who would fall into Jesus' accounting as "those who have nothing," this is a promise we make, both individually and corporately, every time we offer those baptismal vows. We are called to seek justice and peace, to regard all human beings as our neighbors, and to understand (as Augustine said) that we love God most powerfully and tangibly when we express love to our fellow human beings.

About a year before we set off for seminary together, my St. James' friend (now the Reverend) Carissa Baldwin said something to me that was both challenging and true, as Carissa's words often are. "You talk a lot about the poor," she said, and I nodded, maybe even felt good about myself. In writing, in speaking, in prayer, in the occasional sermon I was preaching then, I did advocate for economic justice.

But knowledge and prayer on their own are not enough. "Fine," she went on, "so you talk about the poor. Why don't you *do* something with them?"

Ouch.

Well, there wasn't much to say in response to that. She was right, of course. Short of the occasional bit of spare change to your occasional panhandler, I talked a good game, but I wasn't even close to putting my money where my mouth was. My record was one of sympathy toward my neighbor, but that sympathy had not yet made the jump to life-giving love to my neighbor.

What should I do? Where should I start? Well, Carissa, who had done hands-on work with indigents and undocumented workers in the Rio Grande Valley, had a suggestion for me: Austin Interfaith.

It turns out that there were a lot of Episcopalians already working with Austin Interfaith (our first year in seminary, my entire class would be required to work with AI), and with good reason. Austin Interfaith was peace and justice work that worked. This organization, which grew out of organizing techniques created by the labor activist Saul Alinsky, began with conversations, not with handouts. Instead of being top down impersonal giving—much of the charity I'd seen churches and religious organizations do had been about collecting money to send to poor brown people far far away—this was peace and justice work that treated the poor with dignity and credited them with the ability to know what they needed and how to rank those concerns collectively. After we talked as individuals, one on one, we met as a community so that they could highlight from our conversations the most important issues in their lives.

Maybe they chose lack of food or bad sanitation, maybe their passion was behind controlling busy traffic near the neighborhood school, but the point was that they chose their action agenda, not the organizers and volunteers. In Austin Interfaith, those of us working with the poor were not in charge of something; we were simply working alongside the poor to help them realize their vision, providing assistance as we could, and, strangely enough, getting out of the way more often than not. The culmination of this process was when we brought in elected officials or candidates seeking election for a raucous mass meeting in which the politicians were seated in front of the community and asked, yay or nay, would they support AI's agenda?

Austin Interfaith taught me two things: that I could actively be involved in social justice work, and that it had to be done with the people I wanted to help. (And, okay, a third thing: that I was as likely to be helped and changed as a result of the experience as I was likely to help and change anyone.) As the Reverend Dr. Samuel Lloyd notes, being faithful today is not about setting out a predetermined meal and asking people to eat it. It is, instead, about asking them what they need and orienting the Church to be present where they need presence. It's about asking where God is moving, and running to get in line with that.

So, what do people need?

They need to eat good food and drink clean water.

They need a roof over their heads, a warm place to sleep on a cold night.

They need a job or vocation, something to offer a living wage and give them purpose and dignity.

They need a little beauty in their lives.

They need to know that they are not alone, to know that even in the face of death and despair, God—embodied by the Church—is present, and moving in the world.

And finally, people need to know that even if they are rejected and looked down upon by others because of the color of their skin, or their gender, or their place of origin, or their culture, or their sexual orientation, or their faith, or their lack of faith, or their past lives, or their present life, even if they are outcasts or outlaws—that the Church invites them in the name of the Jesus who loves fiercely and unconditionally. To use the words of the Welsh liturgy of confession and absolution that I love so much at Gladstone's Library, no matter who they are or what they have done, people need to know that they are forgiven, accepted, loved, and welcomed to the feast.

We all know we need to be involved in more than our own petty concerns. It doesn't even require religion to point out that selfishness and greed are bad for us, for others, and for the planet, and the Anglican tradition had a powerful justice component long before the Baptismal Covenant. Anglicans and Episcopalians have long known we were connected to each other, part of a larger fabric of being. In a section on the subject of seeking justice ("whereon not only all our present happiness, but in the kingdom of God our future joy dependeth") the Anglican theologian Richard Hooker argued that "God hath created nothing simply for itself, but each thing in all things, and of every thing each part in other have such interest, that in the whole world nothing is found whereunto

any thing created can say, 'I need thee not.' "[26] It is a slightly more theological way of saying what the great priest, poet, and dean of London's
St. Paul's Cathedral John Donne concluded in one of his Meditations: that
no man (or woman) is an island, that what affects any one of us affects us
all, that the distant church bell tolling isn't pealing out the loss or grief
of someone else. It sounds for every one of us in the entire human family.

To be a part of the Anglican tradition, then, is to recognize that you
are connected to all of humanity and to all of creation. That almost necessarily should call you to be working for peace and justice, and certainly
we have noble examples: William Wilberforce, an evangelical Anglican,
was the primary force behind the abolition of the slave trade in England
(he also supported education for the poor, opposed dueling, and one year
when food was scarce in England, gave away more to charity than his
annual income!). William Gladstone, who wanted to take Anglican holy
orders but instead entered politics and became the greatest statesman
in British history, sought to make his political decisions based on his
very clear religious commitments to justice. It was Gladstone who first
elevated human rights to the status of a political issue, Gladstone and
his wife who scandalized Victorian society by trying to help prostitutes
leave that life, and Gladstone who pushed through legislation offering
education to all children.

Not all Anglicans worked for issues of peace and justice, of course.
Many were content to sit in a pew on Sunday morning and enjoy the
music, and our history on justice issues here in the States is likewise
mixed. Episcopalians divided nationally over the issue of slavery (as did
many denominations), and some were publicly on the wrong side of history on civil rights. Some Episcopalians have preferred to live out their
faith in the pews rather than on the picket line. But the Episcopal Church
also has prophetic figures worth celebrating and emulating. We've mentioned John Hines, that towering figure for racial and economic justice
who was elected presiding bishop in the 1960s, and Jonathan Myrick
Daniels, the Episcopal seminarian who stepped between a young black
girl and a shotgun in Alabama and was killed. In 1991, Daniels was added
to the Church calendar of saints and martyrs, and he is celebrated now
every year on the anniversary of his death—as is non-Episcopalian Martin
Luther King on the anniversary of his.

That calendar of feasts, in fact, is a rainbow of men and women from across the world and from many traditions. What they have in common seems to be that our Church wanted to recognize their importance to our faith and practice. Some are predictable if potent luminaries from our Catholic and Anglican past, but many have been chosen to demonstrate the Church's commitment to justice and diversity. So it is that we commemorate John Donne, but also Oscar Romero, the martyred Catholic bishop from San Salvador. Anthony the Great, the founder of Christian monasticism is honored, but so is Elizabeth Seton, the founder of the Sisters of Mercy. Thomas Becket, the archbishop of Canterbury martyred in Canterbury Cathedral at the behest of King Henry II, is on the list; so is Janani Luwum, the archbishop of Uganda, martyred at the behest of Idi Amin in 1977.

When I joined the Episcopal Church in 2003, I was stunned to discover that David Pendleton Oakerhater, a Cheyenne warrior and Episcopal deacon who ran the Whirlwind Mission a mile from my grandmother's farm in Oklahoma, is on our list. He was, in fact, the first Native American on the saints calendar. But many non-Episcopal men and women are on the list as well. The Catholic saints and scholars, I understand. I could not be a good Episcopalian without Augustine, or Anselm, or Aquinas. I could also understand the great figures of Christian faith—yes, we should honor Martin Luther and Dietrich Bonhoeffer.

But here were the Dorchester Chaplains, too—the Catholic priest, rabbi, Methodist minister, and Reformed minister—who organized the evacuation of their ship when it was torpedoed by a German submarine in 1943, gave up their own life jackets to others, and remained on the sinking ship to pray for those in the icy waters. And here were Sojourner Truth and Harriet Tubman, the great African American abolitionists and women's rights activists, alongside feminists Elizabeth Cady Stanton and Amelia Bloomer, all powerful and brave women being remembered on the same day. And here, wonder of wonders, was Lottie Moon, the Southern Baptist missionary who spent forty years in China, and in whose honor every year in my Baptist church we used to hoard our change for the Lottie Moon Christmas Offering.

What the collection of lesser feasts and fasts teaches us is that the Episcopal Church has chosen to place itself firmly on the side of inclusion, to recognize the spiritual gifts of men and women from many different times, races, faiths, and cultures. In this celebration of the achievements and hardships of men and women from across the centuries, we witness another way in which our commitment to the *via media* also becomes a quest to do justice to the vast range of human experience. When we can say that our lives in Christ could—and perhaps should—be shaped by the examples of all these who have gone before, we are recognizing again the interconnectedness of human experience, one of the prerequisites for true justice.

We have also seen the Episcopal Church's commitment to justice demonstrated by the decisions it has reached on the inclusion of blacks, women, and gays in the Church. One of the things that religion, to its shame, sometimes does is draw lines, but what the Episcopal Church has chosen to do in each of these cases is open doors, often at huge political and institutional costs, as we noted in the chapter on the culture wars.

Episcopal author and activist John Green (author of *The Fault in Our Stars* and other best-selling novels) says that you don't have to be religious to recognize that we have two dueling impulses at work within us—the impulse toward laziness and safety and selfishness that we mostly indulge, and the impulse to do something to make the world a better place, which we should indulge. It's the second impulse we're celebrating in this chapter, that urge to help others, to reduce the level of suffering in the world, to give all people a decent chance at life and happiness.

As Sara Miles notes in *Take This Bread* (and I, with my past history of "talking about the poor" could attest), it is easy to have a vague commitment toward doing the right thing, but what is hard indeed is to make those choices that involve risk. Doing the right thing feels sometimes like a dangerous thing—and sometimes, it actually *is* a dangerous thing. But doing the right thing, seeking justice and offering mercy, is at the core of any authentic faith, Episcopal or otherwise.

The benediction of the Eucharist at Gladstone's Library draws from Micah 6:8 to sum up the requirements of the faithful life:

> This is what God requires of us, only this:
> To do justice,
> love kindness,
> and walk humbly with our God.

St. James' Episcopal in Austin, the African American mission church that chose to welcome people of all races, cultures, and sexual orientations, has never forgotten that this is what God requires. But their rector, the Reverend Lisa Saunders, told me that they were still, after all these years, making a conscious effort to see the connections between being St. James' inside the church and outside the church:

> This year our community is rededicating ourselves to the work of radical welcome and racial reconciliation out in the world. At times we can think that worshipping with a diverse crowd is enough to transform us. Maybe that is true. I believe that by living in community with a diverse body of Christ, we are able to know the other more fully. We are transformed by the truth of the experience of the other. Then, when we leave the walls of our building, we can see the world with new eyes, and use our position to change institutional racism and injustices.

Sara Miles, who came to her Episcopal faith late in life, offers a similar vision when asked what she thinks people should do who want to somehow be Christian, but don't want to do it in the way that American mainstream Christianity seems to demand, a religion of rules, intolerance, and sometimes, injustice. What she offers us feels like a very Episcopal understanding of the place of love, justice, and mercy in our lives. If you want to follow Christ, she says:

> First, *do* something. Feed, heal, help. Don't just argue about ideology. Second, pray for your enemies. Don't pray that they become different, or start doing what you want them to do. Just pray for them.
>
>   You don't get to practice Christianity by hanging out with people who are like you and believe what you believe. You have to rub up against people you think are misguided, dangerous, or just plain wrong.[27]

It all sounds familiar: Jesus gives one commandment in the Gospel of John, although it is the hardest single thing we do in this life: Love each other.

We practice Christianity by loving, not by assent to certain facts about God, not by a certain way of praying or worshipping or believing. That's not what makes us Christian.

They will know we are Christians by our love.

That love is not conditional, and we don't get to pick whom we love, or how much we love them. We are called to love the people with whom we differ. Maybe most especially them. We are called to show that love, tangibly, sometimes sacrificially.

We are called to keep on loving, to love without ceasing.

And ultimately, despite our passion for beautiful liturgy, despite our compassion for those with whom we share our spiritual journey, we are called to get up out of our churches and get back out into the world. "Go in peace," the dismissal tells us, "to love and serve the Lord."

And so we do.

In 2014, as I was writing this book in Wales, a wave of immigrant children was washing against the southern border of the United States, particularly along the border between Mexico and my home state of Texas. Local, state, and national politicians argued about what we should do about these children. Anti-immigration groups attempted to form blockades, or demonstrated to loudly proclaim their disapproval of undocumented immigrants. Still others turned away, shook their heads, shrugged. What could they do?

When some in the United States looked at these children they saw only an issue: a horde of unwanted brown people coming to take the jobs of good Americans, yet another insoluble problem for a nation wrestling with too many already. But when we looked at these children, what many in the Episcopal Church saw were, simply and sadly, children, fleeing from something far worse than disapproving politicians, children who were often arriving here both destitute and hungry.

Ben Sargent, the Pulitzer Prize-winning editorial cartoonist for the *Austin American Statesman*, is also a lay leader at St. David's in Austin. He published a cartoon about how Uncle Sam said he just wanted to send the children home—but when the children thought about home, what they remembered was chaos, violence, and poverty. Other Episcopalians responded to the flood of children by donating food, clothes, and money— or by actually going to the border to meet and feed them, among them Erin Warde and Lisa Saunders. Lisa wrote back to St. James', Austin, about what she had seen, and what their contributions had helped to provide, starting with something as simple as soup:

Soup is what the doctors recommend, as bigger meals were making people ill because of malnourishment and dehydration for possibly days before even entering the border patrol stations. So, the chicken soup is important. And some of the children were very hungry, even crying from hunger when I met them at the Salvation Army stop at Sacred Heart Roman Catholic Church. Children who did not eat vegetables gobbled that chicken and vegetable soup up! Children who were sobbing from hunger stopped crying after a few bites. Mothers who had just given birth on the border received this as a first meal after their strenuous journey and delivering their babies.[20]

Why do we care about peace and justice? Because sometimes serving —or contributing—something as simple as a bowl of soup for a new mother or a hungry child is the most important thing in the world. St. Teresa of Avila prayed that we are called to be the hands of Christ, to do God's work of justice, compassion, and reconciliation in the world:

> Christ has no body now on earth but yours,
> no hands but yours,
> no feet but yours.
> Yours are the eyes through which Christ's compassion
> is to look out to the earth,
> yours are the feet by which He is to go about doing good,
> and yours are the hands by which He is to bless us now.

Sometimes, despite our selfish humanity, we actually do manage to be the hands of Christ for a broken world. When we are—when we reach out to the world in love—we are doing what we are called to do by our Church and by our faith.

It sounds so simple: Love God with all you are and all you have. Love your neighbor, wherever she or he may be.

That is all.

But that is more than enough to keep us busy.

Questions for Discussion

1. What do you know about Episcopalians and race? Since the Church
    has been dominated by white men for most of its history, what do you
    imagine were the tensions about open inclusion of African Americans
    in worship and leadership? How might those tensions vary depend-
    ing on where the churches were located?
2. What do you believe Christianity requires adherents to do? How do
    you see the relative weight of doctrine and actions? How important
    are peace and justice issues in your own life (and faith, if you consider
    yourself a faithful person)?
3. What do you see as the role of saints in Christian life? How can their
    examples inspire our own journeys? Who are the Christians you most
    admire and why?
4. What are some tangible things that you (or you and your community
    of faith) might do to tangibly illustrate God's love and acceptance of
    all people? What would be the challenges? What, for you and your
    family or community, might be the rewards?

For Further Reading

Gardiner H. Shattuck, Jr., *Episcopalians and Race: Civil War to Civil
Rights* (Lexington: University Press of Kentucky, 2000).

A well-written account of the Episcopal Church's struggle with race
written by historian and priest Gardiner Shattuck, this book shows how
the dueling desires to do justice and to remain culturally viable, particularly in the American South, fought for prominence (and perhaps still do!).

Desmond Tutu, *God Has A Dream: A Vision of Hope for Our Time* (New
York: Image, 2004).

Archbishop Tutu writes briefly but beautifully about God's dream of
a cosmos without pain, prejudice, or fear, and how all of us are called to
bring that dream closer to fruition. As someone who himself lived through
difficult but inspiring times, Tutu brings his own notable example of love

and reconciliation to the table; if he can love, forgive, and accept, then certainly we should be able to as well.

Sara Miles, *Take This Bread: A Radical Conversion* (New York: Ballantine, 2008).

Sara Miles writes in her spiritual autobiography that being fed in the sacrament of the Eucharist changed her life and drew her to involve herself and others in the ministry of feeding the poor. The food bank she helped organize at her church in San Francisco transformed her faith, her church, and the lives of many around her. It is a beautifully written and inspiring story.

Reaching Out:
Touching Lives All Week Long

Shortly after I'd begun attending St. James' Episcopal Church in Austin, I e-mailed its rector, Greg Rickel, and asked him if we could meet for coffee during the week. I didn't know whether or not you were supposed to ask a priest to meet outside of church. Although now it seems that almost all my friends are priests, pastors, or bishops, I didn't understand yet how ridiculously busy pastors are with committees, sermon preparation, pastoral visits, hospital emergencies, administrative duties. I just knew that I had a lot of questions, and Greg had come to be the face of St. James' and the Episcopal Church for me, and I needed to talk about what I was going to do next.

So it was that I e-mailed, "Hey, could we have coffee some time?"

And he e-mailed back, "Yes."

So that spring when our schedules coincided and the stars aligned, we sat down outside a Starbucks on North Lamar in Austin, a few blocks from the Texas School for the Blind and Visually Impaired. I had figured this out because I got there early, and because people in dark glasses with canes were tapping their slow way up and down the sidewalk next to the busy street.

I almost didn't recognize Greg at first. I was used to seeing him vested for worship, wearing what I would later learn were an *alb* (a simple white robe), a *stole* (something like a long elaborate scarf), and a *chausable* (which looked to me like a beautifully decorated poncho). I was growing to understand that in the Anglo-Catholic tradition, these vestments, so alien to me as a low-church Protestant, marked the ordained clergy who led worship, but like my students who think I must dress like Dr. Garrett around the clock, I was half-expecting him to be dressed for church, vested for coffee, instead of wearing shorts and sandals, as I discovered he often did.

"Hey, man," he said, smiling and sticking out a hand. Later we would go straight to hugs upon meeting for coffee, but I could not imagine such a monumental step then.

We went through the line. He ordered something; I got a soy chai latte. Then we settled in at a table outside in the sunlight.

Greg was, as ever, squeezing me in between other appointments, but all the same, there was no sense of urgency about him. He took the time to listen to my story of depression, loss, and search, talked with me about St. James' and its history, shared with me some of his own story, told me about his family, and talked with me about what he was reading these days—he was and is a voracious reader.

Although I was paying attention to our conversation, I couldn't help noticing a drama playing out on the very edge of my vision. It's a writer's curse, being able to observe in all directions. A young blind man with a cane had gotten himself a bit muddled in the middle of the broad driveway leading into the strip mall. Now he was tapping in each direction and not finding a boundary, and easing ever closer to busy Lamar Avenue. I was sitting there and noticing, because that is what writers do. They notice things.

But while I was noticing, Greg was seeing. He got up, walked to the young man, spoke to him, offered him his arm. Then he led him not only safely across the driveway, but down to the corner. There, he waited for the light to change, helped the young man across another busy street, and returned some minutes later to our table.

Without a word of comment, without anything to mark what he had done as anything extraordinary, he launched back into what he had been saying. But I marked it.

I don't know if Greg remembers this act, performed so casually it could almost have been without thinking. But I remember thinking that the church in which I had grown up had focused on the state of people's souls, but not on the quality of their lives.

I remember thinking—and this is probably tremendously unfair to the pastors of my youth, and for that I apologize—that I couldn't imagine any of them performing this good deed. Or at least I couldn't imagine it without their trying to slip in the facts of Christian salvation as a condition of their altruism. I remember hearing my preacher talk about the blind leading the blind and getting the impression that it was just fine if they all wound up in a ditch.

The church that I grew up in was very much a physical space. It was a building, or a set of buildings. When we said we were going to "church," what we meant was that we were driving across town to a place. We were a church that thought of itself as a church because of what happened inside the building on a Sunday or a Wednesday night.

What Greg was modeling for me, though, both in agreeing to meet me during the week and in helping a stranger in need, was something brand new, something I was only just learning that Christianity could be. Greg was teaching me about a church that steps outside its walls and touches people all week long, a church that does the right thing, a church that is about building the Kingdom of God rather than about expanding the church roll.

The Reverend Mary Caucutt, a priest in Cody, Wyoming, says that what she celebrates most about being Episcopalian is "reaching out to the world with love," and in this chapter we want to explore additional ways that the Episcopal Church has been and is doing just that. What makes us "church" is larger than the fact of common worship. Although we've talked about being a tradition that gathers around the Book of Common Prayer, I don't want to define Episcopalians solely as people gathering around the altar on Sunday morning. Bishop Andy Doyle would agree with Mary's assertion that we should be about reaching out to the world with love. He has told me that we should measure the ultimate success of the Church not by how many people are in the church building on Sunday morning, but by how successful we are at reaching out to the world all through the week.

If Episcopal theology is incarnational (which it is), then religion should be about daily life, not portioned off into Sunday islands of information, inspiration, or indoctrination. The challenge Bishop Doyle is posing is this: How are we offering touches 24/7 in addition to—or even instead of—a weekly taste of bread and wine? How are Episcopalians developing new forms of social capital in a culture that, as we have seen, has been moving from the communal to the solo? How can we consciously harness what technology and the Spirit are simultaneously making possible in this quest to embrace the world, even if the world remains determinedly outside on the street corner?

The prayer book has suggested for 450 years that in the Anglican tradition, spirituality should be a part of daily life, but how do we offer that daily touch to people who won't do us the favor of coming to church? As we'll see, small groups, nontraditional events, and social media are offering people new ways of being Episcopal. We've decided that if they won't come to us, we will have to go to them, and thankfully, we are discovering that in some ways, the shifts in our culture are helping us to do just that—and to continue being the Church in the doing.

Back in the Introduction, we talked about how sociologist Robert D. Putnam offered his theory of *Bowling Alone* to account for the decline of communal activities in American life. Not just church attendance was suffering, he argued, but all sorts of groups were losing members. He and Lewis M. Feldstein summarized those findings in their follow-up book, *Better Together: Restoring the American Community*. Beginning in the late 1960s, they note

> Americans in massive numbers began to join less, trust less, give less, vote less, and schmooze less. At first, people hardly noticed what was happening, but over the last three decades, involvement in civic associations, participation in public affairs, membership in churches and social clubs and unions, time spent with family and friends and neighbors, philanthropic giving, even simple trust in other people—as well as participation in the eponymous bowling leagues—all have fallen by 25 to 50 percent. A variety of technological and economic and social changes—television, two-career families, urban sprawl, and so on—has rendered obsolete a good share of America's stock of social capital.[29]

Since the Episcopal Church (and every other denomination) began its decline in the midst of this larger loss of social capital, one might logically ask, what (if anything) could the Church do to enlarge our stock of social capital? How could it bridge gaps, reduce loneliness, help people to feel that they are part of something larger than themselves? And how could it do these things not simply to reverse the "decline" in attendance, but because community, hope, and compassion are central values of the Church, and are valuable for their own sake?

Putnam and Feldstein talk about two elements of social capital that seem to be hardwired into what it means to be Episcopalian. Personal interaction, they tell us, leads to trusting relationships and resilient communities. And social capital is generally only developed in pursuit of a goal or a set of common goals. People do not join groups simply for the sake of joining groups. In other words, people have to come together for a reason that makes sense to them, not simply because somebody wants to form them into a community or a congregation.

Samuel Lloyd spoke of how finding common goals is central to the idea of a church continuing to survive and thrive in its mission. The Episcopal Church—if it is going to exist—has to get outside the walls of its churches and speak to those in the larger world. People don't simply show up in church any more, no matter how magnificent the setting, no matter how beautiful the music, no matter how welcoming the people. The Reverend Dr. Lloyd argues that Luke 10 (in which Jesus commissions the disciples to go out, teaching and healing as he has done), has to be our new paradigm as people of faith. "We have to go out and learn from [others] and meet them where they are."[30] Then—and only then—will we know what they want and how we can be engaged in the things that matter to them.

What Greg Rickel and I were doing at a coffee shop—and what I have done in countless meetings with priests, bishops, and parishioners since then—was a one-to-one meeting. Organizing, as my classmates and I learned our first year in seminary with Austin Interfaith, was about relationships. As Sam Lloyd noted, you can't organize people or inspire them to join a community based on your ideas for them. You have to know who they are, find out where their passions lie. Some of the most successful innovations in the Episcopal Church grow directly out of this desire to discover where people's passions lie.

Rebecca Hall, a pioneer in the use of small groups at St. David's, Austin, helped set up rotating groups (called "Journey Groups") and

occasional educational and social events where people met to discuss
elements of interest, including the Bible, movies, parenting, Christian
spirituality, and many other topics. Most of these groups were mod-
erated by laypeople instead of clergy or church staff; many of them
were populated by people who felt more allegiance to the small groups
than they did to St. David's proper. Rebecca notes, "Journey Groups
are definitely a side door into the church for people who are wary or
who are completely unchurched or who have had previous bad experiences with church. I know of numerous people who would never, ever
join the church or go to worship and who are regular Journey Group
participants."

Part of the rationale for offering Journey Groups, of course, was that
they might encourage those people to someday come in the front door;
another rationale was that it would allow participants to feel a stronger
sense of community than our large church might otherwise offer; a third,
which grew organically, was the sense of allowing people to form groups
of which they wanted to be a part. Rebecca said that the process grew out
of trial and error and could not be top-down:

> I created Journey Groups kind of by accident. I just talked to lots
> of people about their interests and what they wanted. They wanted
> to lead groups, but for short periods of time. People wanted to join
> groups, but not indefinitely. And there were *way* more people who
> wanted to lead groups than I had space for, so I created the system
> of having groups four times a year to give everyone a chance to offer
> their group. It worked.
>
> I plan small groups in an organic, ground-up way. I see my job
> as listening to people (laypeople) talk about what they're passionate
> about and then encouraging them to offer this as a small group to
> the parish. So, when people tell me about books they love or topics
> they want to explore, I say, "That sounds great! You should offer a
> Journey Group on that!"

Journey Groups are one of many nontraditional ways in which
Episcopal churches are reaching out to the culture in a new way. These
small groups meet on various days—sometimes Sunday, but often on
other days. They may meet at the church —or they may meet in someone's

home. But they're not "church as usual," and all of the things we'll discuss in this chapter could be described in that way.

Take Theology on Tap, where people gather in a bar or around a pint to hear a speaker and maybe to discuss theology and spirituality as they understand it. While our friends at Wikipedia say that it was begun in a Catholic parish in Chicago some thirty years ago, I first discovered it through the long-running (since 2003) Theology on Tap program offered by the Episcopal Church of the Advent in Boston. Since then, I've attended a number of Theology on Tap events, spoken at my fair share of them, and even helped run one at Austin's great independent bookstore, BookPeople. What I've discovered in all of these experiences is that it brings together church members, friends, and curious bystanders, who are able to interact in a brand new way outside the strictures of formal church—and with the encouragement of ale.

Theology on Tap is a casual setting where people listen with less judgment, talk more authentically about what they're seeing in their own lives, and socialize with people with whom they might not normally be in community. Theology on Tap seems to be particularly good in attracting people who might not normally acknowledge an interest in theology for fear of being evangelized. In our events at BookPeople, with beer provided by a good Episcopal brewery from Houston, many times bookstore staff would linger to talk to me after an event, always offering something about how they volunteered to work the event with some trepidation. Usually another reaction came up: "This wasn't what I thought it was going to be. It was actually pretty cool."

Now, granted, being "cool" probably shouldn't be a motive for churches to do things. But to not be thought of as old-fashioned, judgmental, irrelevant? As the commercial says, "Priceless." Because it is a social event—and because the presence of alcohol seems to promise a different kind of Christianity than many are used to seeing in the media—Theology on Tap, like many of the initiatives in this chapter, offers a wonderful antidote to the misconceptions and fears people may have about Christianity that keep them away from church. Holy things can — and, in my experience, do—happen in pubs, as they can anywhere else that God is moving. There is nothing wrong with broadening our focus or shifting our venues. As the great Anglican scientist Francis Bacon said,

if the mountain will not come to Mohammed, then Mohammed must go
to the mountain.

We are going to the mountain in lots of ways. Take Laundry Love,
which began at an Episcopal parish in California and now is being done
by over seventy churches, mosques, and synagogues. On publicized
nights, volunteers take over a laundromat and offer the homeless and the
working poor laundry detergent, quarters, and often a hot meal or food
from a food bank. It's part of the Church's commitment to social justice,
sure, but it's more than that. Volunteers are also there for conversation
and presence, and they're creating something holy and relational outside
the parameters of Sunday morning. Shannon Kassoff, a lay leader from
Huntington Beach, California, says that Laundry Love:

> is our church. . . . It is probably the best way to be involved in other
> people's lives, not just handing out food in a soup kitchen, or what-
> ever. We get to know them very well, and that's probably the best
> part of this whole deal. . . . This is probably the most meaningful
> thing that we do, because we're taking our love outside of the walls
> of church. . . . Bringing it to the people and sharing what we think
> is an amazing experience, and that's just love.[31]

What happens when Laundry Love is in the house? Communities
happen. Social capital gets formed. Miracles nobody imagined. Here's
how the Huntington Beach Laundry Love website describes what's been
happening there in 2014:

> One of our regular volunteers said of our most recent Laundry Love,
> "This one just blew my mind." We had volunteers from Mariners
> Church, from St John's in Laverne who are wanting to start their
> own Laundry Love, some folks from other Episcopal churches, and a
> regular group of men from the Islamic Center of Orange County. The
> Islamic Center provided the Middle Eastern meal and led the prayer.
> We didn't start out to be interfaith. We didn't start out to be any
> faith, but that's what happened. The structure just started forming,
> the web that holds us grows stronger. When we're there, we don't
> talk about religion. It's more of an experience thing, an opportunity
> to enjoy one another, to get to know the locals and to allow ourselves
> to be of service and to be served. . . .

We got a new neighbor a couple of months ago, a barbershop next door to the laundromat, and even though we can be rather disruptive and take up a fair amount of space, the new owner jumped right in and started offering haircuts to our guests. Shannon once said, "We see a need and we try to fill that need." That's the premise and it seems that it happens spontaneously.

When we began Laundry Love, all we did was provide money and laundry supplies so that people who needed a hand could get their laundry done free. Soon, our services expanded to include a meal, and then groceries became part of the project. We have made friends, watched fortunes change, have seen people who had been living on the streets for years come in, not to do their laundry for free, but to offer donations and lend a hand. Sometimes people stumble on us "accidentally" and fortuitously, when a bit of hard luck has come their way and then a bit of grace.[32]

Grace is another thing that doesn't only happen in church. If we take incarnation seriously, we've agreed that what happens at the altar on Sunday morning is far from the only way that God is being made manifest in the world. Take farmers' markets or other ventures in which Episcopal parishes offer a service and build social capital, but often with a twist of grace. St. Paul's Episcopal Church in DeKalb, Illinois, led by the Reverend Stacy Walker-Frontjes, sponsors the Thrive Neighborhood Market and Community Garden. They sell affordable fresh produce at the market—and on Tuesday nights, a small community gathers to garden. The Reverend Cara Spaccarelli, of Christ Church Capitol Hill in Washington, DC, is taking seriously the church's role in its urban neighborhood, and bringing together families from the church and families from local housing projects for dinner.

Lucinda Laird, dean of the American Cathedral in Paris, told me about the farmers' market sponsored by her previous parish, St. Matthew's in Louisville, Kentucky. The Narthex Farmers' Market is still in existence (selling tomatoes, cucumbers, greens, cabbages, basil, and cut-flower bouquets on the day I checked), and proceeds from the market go toward the church's food bank. Hosting a farmers' market is not in itself a distinction, although it too is certainly a cool idea. "But what sets us off from any other social space?" Lucinda asked me. It has to be something about our ethos, we concluded; we're not just doing this to provide a service, although it does. We're not just doing this because it creates social capital, although it does. We're doing it because it is part of our mission, in this case feeding the hungry and caring for the poor. And when people spend money on food that helps others to eat, we agreed, not only are they given something they need and want, but they're reminded of deeper needs and wants.

Another way this reminder happens is when Episcopalians bring our liturgy into the lives of our cities on Ash Wednesday, one of the holiest days on the Christian calendar. Ashes to Go was begun by the Reverend Teresa K. M. Danieley in St. Louis, when in 2007 she took to a busy street corner in her city to offer the imposition of ashes to passersby. Ashes to Go is now an international phenomenon, and while not everyone I know is in favor of the concept—it *is* fast food liturgy, as its detractors suggest—that's kind of the whole point in a culture where people eat fast food because they don't have time to sit down for a long leisurely meal. I've eschewed the formal Ash Wednesday liturgy for the past couple of years to receive my ashes on the street. I love the long and beautiful liturgy of the Ash Wednesday service, but imposing or receiving ashes on a street corner, as curious people walk by, walk back, and finally ask what's going on—that is something special in its own right.

My wife, Jeanie, comes down to take pictures and as we stand on a busy downtown corner, I've watched our priests and laypeople alike climb into buses and lean into taxicabs to draw the black cross upon a driver's forehead. I've seen lapsed Catholics break into tears at the remembered ritual, the familiar words of imposition: "Remember that you are dust, and to dust you shall return." Children ask their mothers what is happening—and sometimes the mothers lead them over for an explanation. Office workers in dresses and suits and ties walk by, receive ashes, walk on down the street to lunch or back to work.

Does this convey the impact of the Ash Wednesday service going on back in our historic sanctuary? Well, not the same impact, certainly. But here's the hard truth: None of those people receiving ashes on Sixth Street (okay—none of them except possibly for Jeanie and me) were ever going to walk the three blocks up the hill to our church. It's Ashes to Go or no ashes at all. But nonetheless, something happens here that is very much like the Ash Wednesday miracle that the great Catholic novelist Walker Percy describes at the climax of his novel *The Moviegoer*: "Through some dim dazzling trick of grace," God is present on the corner of Sixth and Congress.[33] Jeanie and I have agreed that Ashes to Go makes us proud to be members of our church. It says something about who we are when we go out to engage the world with what God has given us.

These are tangible offerings, of course, outside the walls, face-to-face meetings where theology is discussed or ritual offered. But these days, not all grace is face to face. Meredith Gould spoke in our chapter on evangelism about virtual meetings in which she saw God moving, and in which our Church should be at the forefront. Our use of social media can be another way that the contemporary Episcopal Church reaches out to the world every day. Jeanie says that social media can serve a number of functions for us, and that it should be taken seriously as a medium for ministry: "Honestly, I think it can replace most things. Conversation—real and intimate—happens over social media. It may not always be kind, but it's real. If you're homebound, completely incapable of doing anything but sitting in a wheelchair with a ventilator, this is a *very* real world full of conversation, connecting, and learning about people." Social media offers, as Meredith noted, a way of interacting that is unmediated, of accessing faith without having to come inside the church. It doesn't have to be— and often isn't—top-down communication, but simply people talking to each other, sharing themselves and those real conversations.

In her book *Social Media Gospel*, Meredith suggests ways that various forms of social media can be used by the Church, and ways they probably can't. They probably can't, for example, replace the experience of hearing a sermon with a group of people at the moment it's first delivered (although you can stream sermons online, send them out in e-mail blasts, publish them on blogs and in Facebook notes, tease them in tweets, post, I suppose, a picture of me preaching to Instagram or Pinterest). Nor can you offer someone bread and wine through your smart phone. But you can preview, review, host discussions, remind people of occasions, offer chances to interact, and create a community that is real and viable through social media. Meredith told me, "Those of us who are passionate about using social media in the context of church and faith do not view it as a substitute or replacement for face-to-face, ITF (In The Flesh. . . . we're not using IRL anymore) community. We view it as a way to supplement and support—providing information, education, and inspiration through another means that is, as I mentioned above, not constrained by time, space, place, or denomination." It's a new world. Too new for some. Meredith tells me she spends much of her time consulting with people who really don't want to use social media in ministry!

What does a new world look like where Episcopalians are worrying less about *doing* church—even for all of us who are fueled by liturgy and music and the community that forms within the walls on Sundays—than they are *being* church? I want to submit that maybe it looks like the life and work of the Episcopal author and activist John Green, who is one of the most popular young adult novelists in America. His best known book, *The Fault in Our Stars*, is about two teens who meet and fall in love at a cancer support group held in the basement of an Episcopal Church, and Green has talked about how the book grew out of the five months he spent as a chaplain in a children's hospital.

Green, in fact, was doing chaplaincy as part of his discernment for the Episcopal priesthood—that is, he and the Church were in the process of deciding whether he should go to seminary and become a priest. He had enrolled in the University of Chicago Divinity School, but his time doing Clinical Pastoral Education (the program in which he served as a student chaplain) convinced him that he would not make a good pastor, and that perhaps his gifts were better used elsewhere.

He still loves the Church, though. You can hear it when he explains to people outside the tradition that priests in the Episcopal Church "can marry and stuff, and they can be ladies. They can be gay. They can be all the things that, you know, humans are."[34] Maybe it's true he decided not to go into seminary and on to formal ministry, but, as Michele Dean puts it in *The New Yorker*, "you could say that, in his career as a young-adult novelist, he's become another sort of evangelist."[35]

Or, as we might say, using language more appropriate to our tradition, another sort of priest. While John Green chose not to be a church leader standing in a pulpit or at an altar inside a church, in a very real sense he is serving as a priest for a huge community of readers, viewers, and activists who have gathered around his work and a thoughtful, engaged, communal desire to make the world a better place—to "decrease suck," as he and members of his "nerdfighter" community would put it.

If you look at the statistics, John Green has more influence and reaches more people now than he ever could have as a priest. In fact, it's hard to imagine any other Episcopalian having the same sort of cultural and social currency that Green has today, although his lessons are lessons we could learn if we haven't yet. He's a compelling storyteller, he engages powerful issues of the day as well as personal issues we all face, he creates room for people to think and feel and talk to each other, and he uses social media with skill to help reach out to people 24/7. Here's a look at the numbers: *The Fault in Our Stars* has sold over ten million copies; the videos made by him and his brother Hank and posted on various nerdfighter YouTube channels have had almost one *billion* views as of the writing of this book (the single short vlog [video blog] post "On Religion" alone has had 887,000 viewers); he has almost three million followers on Twitter and over two million fans on Facebook.

While John Green's work is wildly popular and he is a likeable personality, his popularity is also connected to the creation of social currency. The nerdfighter community, linked largely through social media and shared stories, nonetheless do almost all the things that we say "church" is supposed to do. They support and love each other, they teach each other how to be better humans, and they join together to do good work. Nerdfighters raise money for projects that will reduce world suck, and they carry out projects on their own, inspired by their community. So on the one hand, you might have the larger community raising money for Save the Children; on the other, you might have individual "members" giving people kites and wishing them a nice day.

All of this looks familiar: the connection, the call to live better and truer lives, the recognition that (as good Episcopalians know) it's more important that we be working and hoping together than that we stop to puzzle out all the theology behind it. Green says that he doesn't find the theological wrangling very interesting anyway; in that "On Religion" video, he says that he fears debating the existence of God is an excuse to avoid making the world better, and he tells a story: If you're in a burning house and you hear a voice shouting through the smoke, "Get out of there!", are you going to spend time debating whether it's God or a firefighter talking to you? Or are you just going to get out of the house?[36]

What John Green does say, though, is this: Reflecting on his time as a chaplain, and as an aspirant for holy orders in the Episcopal Church,

> all that stuff I did has been incredibly useful to me as a person, in terms of thinking about how we care for other people. . . . What is really interesting to me is the opportunity to care for people and to think about how best to care for people, how most respectfully to care for people. . . . What helps and what doesn't, what questions are the right questions and what questions are the wrong questions.[37]

There's something very Episcopalian about that formulation, and not only does John regularly and publicly claim his Episcopal faith, not only does he make beautiful art that wrestles with the big questions, not only is he helping to create these virtual and actual communities built around mutual support and care for each other, and doing peace and justice, but he's even created a sort of contemporary litany with manual actions, catchphrases, and "gang signs" that people around the world know, use, and value. I'm drawn in particular to the nerdfighter catchphrase "Don't forget to be awesome" (DFTBA). "Don't forget to be awesome," coming as it usually does at the end of one of his videos, focuses us back on our work in the world just like the dismissal in our church services.

It feels like some hip and beautiful new Episcopal liturgy.

Whatever it is the Church is going to look, sound, and act like in years to come, I am hoping that one of our models will be the work of John Green, who knows what it means to touch people all week long.

Given the way our culture has fragmented and our own selfish desires pull us apart, it's hard to imagine anything reversing the slow decline of our Church, and of all organized religion, and, for that matter, of bowling leagues. But what Laundry Love and Ashes to Go and John Green have in common is considerable, and not just that they all offer us evidence that substantial and growing numbers of people want to feel that they are part of something bigger than themselves. They also show us that the model that has always been our model, God reaching out in love to a broken and hurting world, remains as valid today as it did when the Church began. They show us that with initiative and hard work, we can join with those who know, deep in their hearts, that we are the ones who are going to make the world better through our acts of compassion and justice, through our attempts to create communities that love and support each other in this very hard task of being human.

My Church is not dying. I don't care if it never again has as many Episcopalians on the rolls as in the glory days. What matters is what we Episcopalians now are doing—and how we are reaching out into the world and working to build the Kingdom of God.

And that is as it should be.

Seven years ago this summer, the Reverend David Boyd, Rector of St. David's, Austin, asked me to talk about serving with him and his staff as a lay preacher. I had just graduated from seminary, and I knew that I was not going to be ordained a priest of the Church. That was both a hard and a comforting thing. It was hard because I had trained for it and a part of me felt called to it. A part of me *still* feels called to it. It was comforting because I knew I was a writer and a teacher, and that if I had something to offer the Church that had rescued me it was those gifts, not church administration or conflict resolution or the ability to fix a flooding toilet in the day school.

I thought that the rector of one of the largest Episcopal churches in Texas might talk to me about the many ministries his church was involved in, the chance to have an impact on a substantial number of lives. But when David sat down with me, he didn't say, "I want you to come to St. David's to preach great sermons and pack the pews on Sunday morning." He didn't say, "I want you to come to St. David's and teach classes that will bring in people from all over town." He didn't say, "I want you to come to St. David's and write books and get our name out there where it might bring people in here."

No. He looked at me, and he smiled, and he gently offered me an invitation that wasn't about his church, or even the Church, but was exactly the invitation I needed. "I'd like you to come to St. David's," he said to me, "and help us build the Kingdom."

That is what we have done. And that is what all of us are doing. It is why my hope for the Church has never been higher. Episcopalians are building the Kingdom of God with beautiful worship and daily prayer. They are building the Kingdom of God by being welcoming and reconciling communities. They are building the Kingdom of God by marching against the death penalty and by speaking out against intolerance. They are building the Kingdom with their money and their time. They are building the Kingdom with soup kitchens and with homeless shelters. They are building the Kingdom with community gardens and Ashes to Go. They are building the Kingdom by offering a countercultural example. They are building the Kingdom one tweet at a time. And they are doing all this, not because it pads our church attendance, but because it is the thing we are called to do.

"Of course the Church is not dying," David Sugeno said. "That is one of my most deeply held assumptions. How can we who have died and discovered new life believe that for a second?"

We will never dominate American life as we once did, thank God, although I think we can still exercise a substantial influence on our culture. But even if someday all of us Episcopalians were able to fit into a laundromat, I would not despair. If so, we would just invite others to the feast, hand out detergent and quarters, and praise God, from whom all blessings flow.

So here's our challenge: danger and opportunity walking hand in hand, a world full of people waiting to be invited into relationship with us and with the God who created and loved us.

Don't forget to be awesome.

Questions for Discussion

1. What does it mean to you to be invited to *be* church rather than *do* church? How might that change your practice or the practice of your community?
2. How does the Book of Common Prayer orient us toward the world outside our walls? What parts of our liturgy in prayer and worship are about what happens after we experience them in church?
3. Do any of the missional opportunities discussed in this chapter interest you? Is your community of faith already doing one or more of them? If so, what has your experience of them been?

4. How does a notion of directing our attention outward rather than inward change the culture of the Episcopal Church? How would it change the culture of your church?

For Further Reading

Andrew Doyle, *Unabashedly Episcopalian: Proclaiming the Good News of the Episcopal Church* (New York: Morehouse, 2012).

The bishop of Texas (and one of the youngest and most innovative bishops in the Episcopal Church) discusses his vision of Episcopal belief and practice by exploring one of our most important touchstones as Episcopalians, the Baptismal Covenant in the Book of Common Prayer, which he says launches us back outside the Church.

Meredith Gould, *The Social Media Gospel: Sharing the Good News in New Ways* (Collegeville, MN: Liturgical Press, 2013).

This Episcopal lay leader and technology guru expertly explains the strengths and weaknesses of various forms of social media as she makes her case for incorporating social media into any contemporary ministry seeking to reach people in their daily lives.

John Green, http://johngreenbooks.com

The website of popular Episcopal writer John Green offers reflections on matters of the day, links to his weblog and other sites, and a sense of the community forming around him and his works. You may find the "Frequently Asked Questions" page particularly interesting!

Author's Note

This book uses a minimum of footnotes. Although I've done a great deal of reading and research, I wanted to make the text as readable as possible, so I wanted to cut distractions like notes to a minimum. The many unreferenced quotations and summaries you see here are drawn from live, phone, and e-mail conversations, from text messages, and from Facebook posts and messages. They represent the much larger sampling of responses that emerged in my writing and research.

I offer my sincere thanks to all those from across the Episcopal Church and the Anglican world who responded to my queries and who shared stories of their fears, hopes, dreams, and love for the Church. To know that so many people remain as passionate as I am about the Episcopal Church—and that they see it continuing into the far future—made writing this book a joy. It was an outpouring of thought and opinion that I have tried to honor by making these responses the center of this book.

I thank my community of faith, St. David's Episcopal Church in Austin, Texas, its rector, the Reverend David Boyd, and all the priests, staff, and parishioners alongside whom I have been honored to serve. I thank St. James', Austin, for rescuing me and sending me back out into the world, and Calvary, Bastrop, for teaching me many things, and for bearing with my learning on such a public stage. I also must thank the many churches (Episcopal and otherwise!) where I have spoken, preached, or worshipped in the past ten years. I have learned from and been shaped by every one of them.

I give thanks to Baylor University, where I have been upheld in my writing, preaching, and speaking by the administration and my colleagues. Baylor's support for Christian scholarship distinguishes it, and I am honored to be a member of the faculty. A special thank you to my colleague the Reverend Hulitt Gloer, who offered his cabin as a writing refuge as I was working on this book, and his ongoing friendship and assistance whenever I puzzled over it.

I thank the Episcopal Seminary of the Southwest, which trained me, offered an early public forum to discuss the issues raised in this book, and provided the office in which I researched and wrote much of this book. Dean Cynthia Briggs Kittredge and Academic Dean Scott Bader-Saye saw this book as a service to the Church and helped me in every way they could. Anthony Baker taught me theology, and continues to teach me. And three of my seminary professors, now retired, shaped this book in significant ways. I offer my thanks and the deepest respect to the Reverends Charlie Cook, Bill Adams, and Roger Paynter.

I thank Gladstone's Library in Hawarden, Wales, and its warden, the Reverend Peter Francis, for the scholarship that allowed me to finish this book in residence at the library. Gladstone's is a credit to its great Anglican founder, and one of the world's shining lights of learning.

I am thankful to the Right Reverend Greg Rickel for writing the beautiful Foreword to this book, for his service to the Church we both love, and for our years of friendship and conversation. I am grateful for the Right Reverend Andy Doyle's engagement with my life and work, and am privileged to have him as my bishop. I am likewise indebted for the friendship of the Right Reverend Rowan Williams, who continues to be a voice of wisdom in my life and in the life of the Church.

I am grateful beyond words for my wife, Jeanie, and for our children, Jake, Chandler, Lily, and Sophia, all of whom manifest God's love to me every day of my life.

And above all, I am grateful for that God, the Creator, Redeemer, and Sustainer, whose Church can never die. May this book be a suitable offering.

Greg Garrett
Gladstone's Library
Hawarden, Cymru
Ordinary Time
August, 2014

Notes

1. Edward Gibbon, *The Decline and Fall of the Roman Empire* (vol. 1, 1896; London: Methuen & Co., 1909), 1.

2. The Rev. Thomas Brackett, "Postcards from the Edge of Ministry," Blandy Lecture, Seminary of the Southwest, Austin, Texas, Sept. 17, 2013.

3. Victoria de Csillery, "Tools for Prayer," *Trinite,* Fall 2012, 16.

4. James Wood, "God Talk: The Book of Common Prayer at three hundred and fifty," *The New Yorker*, October 22, 2012. Accessed at: http://www.new yorker.com/magazine/2012/10/22/god-talk

5. Benedicta Ward, ed., *The Sayings of the Desert Fathers* (Kalamazoo, MI: Cistercian Press, 1984), 3.

6. Tom Wright, *Simply Christian: Why Christianity Makes Sense* (London: SPCK, 2006), 142.

7. *Ibid.*, 157.

8. Martyn Percy, *Thirty Nine New Articles: An Anglican Landscape of Faith* (London: Canterbury Press Norwich, 2013), 22.

9. "February 2 is Theological Education Sunday," *The Episcopal Church,* January 31, 2014. Accessed at: http://www.episcopalchurch.org/notice/february -2-theological-education-sunday

10. George R. R. Martin, *A Clash of Kings* (1999; New York: Bantam, 2012), 813–14.

11. Lillian Daniel, "Spiritual But Not Religious? Please Stop Boring Me," *The Huffington Post*, September 13, 2011. Accessed at: http://www.huffingtonpost .com/lillian-daniel/spiritual-but-not-religio_b_959216.html

12. Alain de Botton, *Religion for Atheists: A Non-believer's Guide to the Uses of Religion* (New York: Pantheon, 2012), 37.

13. Wright, *Simply Christian*, 180.

14. Rowan Williams, *Tokens of Trust: An Introduction to Christian Belief* (London: Canterbury Press Norwich, 2007), 99–100.

15. Sara Miles, *Take This Bread: A Radical Conversion* (London: Canterbury Press Norwich, 2008), xiv.

16. Richard Harries, *Art and the Beauty of God: A Christian Understanding* (London: Mowbray, 1993), 6.

17. Rowan Williams, *Grace and Necessity: Reflections on Art and Love* (London: Morehouse, 2005), 94.

18. Barbara Brown Taylor, *An Altar in the World: Finding the Sacred Beneath Our Feet* (London: Canterbury Press Norwich, 2009), xv.

19. Alan Ball, *American Beauty*, 1999.

20. You may read Bob's original essay and see his pictures of the first same-sex blessing in Texas at bobkinney.wordpress.com. Type "first blessing gay union texas" in the search box.

21. Katie Sherrod, "Bumper sticker ministry," *Desert's Child*, June 21, 2013. Accessed at: http://wildernessgarden.blogspot.co.uk/2013/06/bumper-sticker -ministry.html

22. The Rev. Dr. Samuel Lloyd III, "All Things New," Harvey Lecture, Seminary of the Southwest, Austin, Texas, March 24, 2014.

23. Francis of Assisi, *First Rule of the Friars Minor*, Chapter 17.

24. "Hurricane Katrina: A message from the Presiding Bishop," Episcopal News Service, August 31, 2005. Accessed at: http://archive.episcopalchurch.org /3577_64601_ENG_HTM.htm

25. Miles, *Take This Bread*, 93.

26. Richard Hooker, *The Works of Mr. Richard Hooker*, vol. III, John Keble, ed. (Oxford: Oxford University Press, 1888), 617.

27. Miles, *Take This Bread*, 289.

28. *News from St. James* July 31, 2014. Accessed at: http://myemail.constant contact.com/News-from-St-James-.html?soid=1101547717648&aid=RFe5UJbuGuE

29. Robert D. Putnam and Lewis M. Feldstein with Don Cohen, *Better Together: Restoring the American Community* (New York: Simon and Schuster, 2003), 4.

30. The Rev. Dr. Samuel Lloyd III, "All Things New."

31. Lisa Napoli, "A Growing Movement to Spread Faith, Love—And Clean Laundry," NPR, July 27, 2014. Accessed at: http://www.npr.org/2014 /07/27/335290086/a-growing-movement-to-spread-faith-love-and-clean -laundry

32. *Laundry Love Project HB*. Accessed August 13, 2014 at: http://www .laundrylovehb.com

33. Walker Percy, *The Moviegoer* (1961; New York: Random House, 1988), 235.

34. John Green, "Hospital Chaplain: The Miracle of Swindon Town #33," *YouTube*, November 2, 2011. Accessed at: https://www.youtube.com/watch ?v=1udWGw7KsIc

35. Michelle Dean, "A Note on Nerdfighters," *The New Yorker*. Accessed March 13, 2013, at: http://www.newyorker.com/culture/culture-desk /a-note-on-nerdfighters   .

36. John Green, "On Religion," *YouTube*, June 20, 2011. Accessed at: https:// www.youtube.com/watch?v=hXlI8Wn8J3Q

37. John Green, "Hospital Chaplain: The Miracle of Swindon Town #33."

About the Author

Greg Garrett, Ph.D., "one of America's leading voices on religion and culture" (BBC Radio), is the author or co-author of twenty books of fiction, memoir, criticism, and theology. These include *The Other Jesus, The Gospel according to Hollywood, Stories from the Edge: A Theology of Grief, We Get to Carry Each Other: The Gospel according to U2, Entertaining Judgment: The Afterlife in Popular Imagination*, and the novel *The Prodigal*, co-written with Brennan Manning. He also writes regularly for print and web publications including *The Huffington Post, Patheos, OnFaith, The Washington Post*, and *Reform* (UK).

Greg serves as 2013 Centennial Professor at Baylor University, where he teaches classes in creative writing, film, literature, and theology. He also serves as Writer in Residence at the Episcopal Theological Seminary of the Southwest, Residential Scholar at Gladstone's Library in Hawarden, Wales, and as a licensed lay preacher based at St. David's Episcopal Church in Austin, Texas. He lives in Austin with his wife, Jeanie, and their children, Jake, Chandler, Lily, and Sophie.